Tailoring Medical Standards for Air Force Personnel

SEAN ROBSON, MARIA C. LYTELL, MIRIAM MATTHEWS, CARRA S. SIMS,
TRACY C. KRUEGER, SPENCER R. CASE, KATHERINE COSTELLO,
SYDNE NEWBERRY

Prepared for the Department of the Air Force
Approved for public release; distribution unlimited

RAND PROJECT AIR FORCE

For more information on this publication, visit www.rand.org/t/RRA571-1

Library of Congress Cataloging-in-Publication Data is available for this publication.
ISBN: 978-1-9774-0659-0

Preface

To serve in the U.S. military, individuals must meet medical standards to ensure that they are fit to serve. The minimum medical standards are set by the U.S. Department of Defense, and the individual services establish additional standards for specific career fields or occupational categories. To ensure that the Department of the Air Force can access and maintain personnel in critical skill areas, the Office of the Surgeon General in the U.S. Air Force expressed interest in exploring alternative ways to use medical standards and employ new methods to help assess and align personnel to career fields and jobs. This report explores the cultural implications of tailoring medical standards to expand—or limit—the pool of qualified personnel to Air Force culture.

This report describes work that should be of interest to military policymakers and researchers involved in setting and evaluating military medical standards and selection processes. The research reported here was commissioned by Major General Robert I. Miller and conducted within the Manpower, Personnel, and Training Program of RAND Project AIR FORCE as part of a fiscal year 2018 project, "Recruit, Train, and Retain Mission-Capable Airmen: Current Practices & Future Perspectives."

RAND Project AIR FORCE

RAND Project AIR FORCE (PAF), a division of the RAND Corporation, is the Department of the Air Force's (DAF's) federally funded research and development center for studies and analyses, supporting both the United States Air Force and the United States Space Force. PAF provides DAF with independent analyses of policy alternatives affecting the development, employment, combat readiness, and support of current and future air, space, and cyber forces. Research is conducted in four programs: Strategy and Doctrine; Force Modernization and Employment; Manpower, Personnel, and Training; and Resource Management. The research reported here was prepared under contract FA7014-16-D-1000.

Additional information about PAF is available on our website: www.rand.org/paf/

This report documents work originally shared with DAF on September 7, 2018. The draft report, issued on September 27, 2018, was reviewed by formal peer reviewers and DAF subject-matter experts.

Contents

Figures

Tables

Summary

Issue

Service members must meet medical standards set by the U.S. Department of Defense (DoD) to ensure that they are fit to serve in the U.S. military (see Figure S.1). However, the individual services establish additional standards for specific career field categories. To ensure that critical skill needs are met in the future, the Department of the Air Force is interested in better ways to assess and align personnel to career fields and asked RAND Project AIR FORCE to explore the use of medical standards for such purposes, including the social implications to Air Force culture.

Approach

The study team used weight and hearing standards to illustrate options for tailoring servicewide medical standards. To gauge support for tailored standards, the team held focused discussions with 25 stakeholders, including 14 from three specialty areas: cyber, aircraft maintenance, and remotely piloted aircraft. In addition, the team developed and conducted a survey focused on potential barriers in Air Force culture to implementing tailored weight and hearing standards for airmen in cyber career fields—highly technical career fields with fewer physical demands. The survey also addressed perceptions related to other medical conditions (such as asthma or depression) and potential uses for genetic testing.

Figure S.1. Overview of Key Factors for Medical Standards in the Military

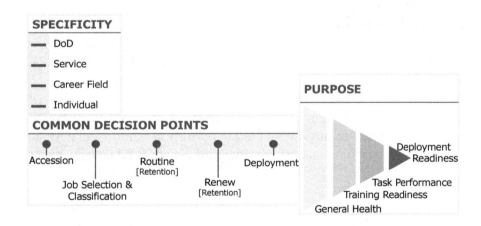

NOTE: Medical standards are used for screening purposes throughout an airman's career. These standards help determine whether airmen meet general health requirements for accession and retention, whether an airman is capable of performing required tasks for job selection and classification, and whether an airman is ready for training or deployment. Policies are set by DoD, by the services, and for individual career fields or communities. Collectively, these policies determine the qualification of individual airmen at different points in their careers.

Findings

- DoD policies on medical standards might present policy barriers to Air Force–tailored medical standards—limiting the degree to which standards could be relaxed.
- In general, subject-matter experts questioned the value of tailoring medical standards.

  - Requirements for deployment serve as a significant barrier.
  - The need for tailored medical standards was not apparent; experts cited the waiver process as having sufficient flexibility to tailor standards to individual cases.
  - Airmen in leadership positions who have met relaxed standards might not be perceived as effective or command respect.
  - Lowering standards might result in lower acceptance of coworkers.

- Survey findings revealed potential cultural barriers and suggest that relaxing medical standards might not be equally accepted by airmen.

  - Perceptions toward airmen not meeting weight standards were more negative than toward those with hearing conditions.
  - Concerns about overweight coworkers related to perceptions of fairness (the need for accommodation), stereotypes, and the ability to maintain self-discipline.
  - Concerns about hearing impairment focused on performance, safety, and putting coworkers at risk.

- Airmen were not fully supportive of the use of genetic testing for purposes outside communicating potential genetic conditions.

Recommendations

- *Proceed carefully with any plans to further implement biomarkers into the accession process.* First, consider a voluntary program on a trial basis that would use results to inform applicants of health risks but not to influence selection, classification, or other personnel decisions.
- *Balance potential concerns about fairness with underlying cultural concerns when considering policy changes.* Communication, systematic and transparent decisionmaking, and training and education would be essential to implementing tailored medical standards.
- *Evaluate the potential benefits and consequences of a fully tailored medical standard.* Before pursuing the implementation of tailored standards, use trial tests with various options, such as limited-term waivers for a temporary condition and permanent waivers for a permanent condition, to assess the potential benefits and consequences.

Acknowledgments

Many people made this project a success. We begin by thanking our sponsors, Maj Gen Roosevelt Allen, who served as our original sponsor until his retirement, and Maj Gen Robert Miller, his successor. We also express gratitude to our action officers, Col Martin LaFrance and Clifford Otte, who assisted our efforts. We also thank Col Daniel Shore for his valuable input on the objective and scope of the project.

Several individuals throughout the Air Force deserve our gratitude. We thank Col (Ret.) Hernando Ortega for spending time explaining Air Force medical policy and practice to the team and providing valuable documentation for our policy review. We also thank CMSgt Greg Gehron, James Rector, and Stephen Poppendieck for their support in coordinating and executing the surveys at Keesler Air Force Base.

We also extend our gratitude to the airmen who took time out of their day to complete the cultural acceptability surveys and to the experts who participated in our interviews. We learned valuable information about the opportunities and challenges of tailoring medical standards from the survey and interview participants.

We also thank several of our RAND Corporation colleagues. We thank Tetsuhiro Yamada for providing background on the civilian literature on selection and screening. We thank Ray Conley, former director of RAND Project AIR FORCE's Manpower, Personnel, and Training Program, for his guidance and support throughout the project. We also appreciate John Crown for his initial guidance on policy and several other researchers who contributed to the broader project objectives, including Brandon Crosby, Paul Emslie, Chaitra Hardison, David Schulker, and Matt Walsh. We express our sincere gratitude to Karin Liu and Ryan McKay from the RAND Survey Research Group for programming the survey forms and also inputting and formatting the survey data. We also thank Zack Steinborn for taking notes during interviews and Pardee RAND Graduate School students who helped review the survey content: John Hamm, Benjamin Goirigolzarri, Felix Knutson, Jake McKeon, and Russ Williams. Finally, we would like to thank our reviewers, including Marek Posard, Ed Chan, and Deborah Gebhardt.

Abbreviations

AC	abdominal circumference
ADHD	attention deficit hyperactivity disorder
AFI	Air Force Instruction
AFRS	Air Force Recruiting Service
AFSC	Air Force Specialty Code
ANG	Air National Guard
BMT	basic military training
COCOM	combatant command
DoD	U.S. Department of Defense
DoDI	Department of Defense Instruction
MEPS	Military Entry Processing Station
MSD	Medical Standards Directory
OSD P&R	Office of the Under Secretary of Defense for Personnel and Readiness
PAF	RAND Project AIR FORCE
PFT	Physical Fitness Test
PTSD	posttraumatic stress disorder
PULHES	Physical Profile Serial Chart
RPA	remotely piloted aircraft
SAT	Strength Aptitude Test
SME	subject-matter expert

1. Introduction and Background

To serve in the U.S. military, applicants must meet medical and physical standards that ensure that they are fit for service.[1] The U.S. Department of Defense (DoD) establishes "the medical conditions and physical defects that are causes for rejection for military service" in policy, specifically DoD Instruction (DoDI) 6130.03 (Air Force Instruction [AFI] 48-123, 2018). The medical and physical conditions referenced by this policy are a frequent cause for disqualification of potential military recruits. Between 2010 and 2015, about 20 percent of enlisted applicants initially were medically disqualified to serve. Reasons for medical disqualifications at entry vary, but the top three categories of medical disqualifications for enlisted applicants from 2010 to 2015 are (1) weight and body build, (2) refraction (i.e., visual impairment), and (3) psychiatric (Boivin et al., 2016).

To ensure that critical skill needs are met in the future, the U.S. Air Force is interested in better ways to assess and align personnel to career fields. Part of that interest focuses on tailoring medical standards to meet the needs of career fields. Tailoring medical standards involves the systematic development of alternative standards (or tests) or exemptions for one or more medical conditions for individuals or groups of individuals who otherwise meet all other requirements for military service. Although tailoring medical standards may help the Air Force and specific career fields meet manpower requirements, such changes may not be uniformly supported across the Air Force. Given these concerns, the Air Force asked RAND Project AIR FORCE (PAF) to explore alternative ways to assess and align personnel to career fields and jobs using medical standards. As part of this project, the RAND PAF team developed a risk assessment framework for medical standards, conducted a simulation using personnel data, and examined potential cultural barriers that could affect the successful implementation of tailored medical standards. This report describes the analysis of cultural barriers, which can limit the effectiveness of any effort to tailor medical standards.

Study Approach

This report describes our approach, findings, and recommendations aimed to help the Air Force identify options to address the potential benefits and costs of tailored medical standards.

The Office of the Air Force Surgeon General asked RAND to address three primary questions:

---

[1] Title 10 of the U.S. Code (USC) specifies that the service secretaries (e.g., Secretary of the Air Force) may accept enlistments (per § 505) who are "qualified, effective, and able-bodied persons . . . " (p. 257). For commissioning officers, 10 USC § 532 specifies that an original appointment to commission into the Regular Air Force requires that the applicant, among other things, is "physically qualified for active service" (p. 327).

1. What are the social issues specific to the Air Force's culture to consider when tailoring medical standards?
2. What other barriers may affect implementation of tailored medical standards?
3. What options can the Air Force consider to address cultural barriers to tailoring medical standards?

To address these questions, we performed several tasks with a focus on weight as a way to illustrate concepts and options for tailoring standards. Being overweight[2] has been identified as a significant barrier to eligibility for military service for both men and women (Cawley and Maclean, 2012). Moreover, growing concerns over obesity in the United States prompted a formal review of recruitment policies and standards related to weight (Centers for Disease Control and Prevention, 2020; Dall et al., 2007; Defense Health Board, 2013; Reyes-Guzman et al., 2015). Although the Defense Health Board found that current standards are appropriate, it also concluded that a "lack of data regarding those who are turned away from recruitment centers because of overweight and obesity indicators creates challenges in assessing the actual recruitment losses related to these factors" (Defense Health Board, 2013, p. 3). Given these concerns, weight serves as a useful example for this project. In addition to weight, we also use hearing impairment as an example in select analyses to illustrate a medical condition that is less controllable, often permanent, and less observable. The following two sections provide more details about our approach, and we conclude with a short section discussing limitations.

Interviews and Surveys to Identify Cultural Barriers to Use of Tailored Medical Standards

A central concern of tailoring standards for any service, career field, or individual is that such changes may not be uniformly supported. To address this concern, we held a small number of focused discussions with stakeholders representing relevant perspectives, including recruiting, selection policy, medical standards, and career field management representing three specialty areas: cyber, aircraft maintenance, and remotely piloted aircraft (RPA). In addition to these discussions, we developed and conducted a survey focused on potential cultural barriers to implementing tailored weight and hearing standards for airmen in cyber career fields. The cyber career field was selected based on preliminary discussions with the sponsor's office to focus efforts on a career field that is technical but may have fewer physical demands compared with other career fields (e.g., maintenance). To a limited extent, the survey also addressed a few other topic areas, including perceptions related to other medical conditions (e.g., asthma, depression) and potential uses for genetic testing (e.g., to screen recruits). The genetic testing portion of the

---

[2] *Overweight* is defined as "E1.1.9. Overweight. A Service member whose body weight exceeds the maximum limit indicated in the Service height to weight screening table. Members who exceed the weight screen may still comply with fitness and general health standards if they meet body fat standards" (DoDI 1308.3, 2002, p. 10).

survey included exploratory items to address alternative tests that could potentially be available to the Air Force in the future to screen and classify airmen.

Certain Limitations Are Associated with the Interviews and Survey Results

The survey results provide examples of the types of cultural barriers that may need to be addressed to successfully implement tailored medical standards. That said, there are important limitations to consider when interpreting the results. Specifically, the interviews and survey results represent a relatively small cross-section of the Air Force at one point in time—559 airmen in cyber-related career field training.[3] Survey respondents consisted of trainees attending cyber-related courses at one point in time. Therefore, the results reflect the attitudes of survey respondents only and are not generalizable to other airmen. Moreover, the subject-matter experts (SMEs) we interviewed did not represent a broad sample of Air Force Specialty Codes (AFSCs). Notwithstanding these limitations, the analytic approach provides a useful demonstration for how the Air Force could augment existing data to support medical standards decisionmaking. Finally, it is important to note that the types of biases and perceptions explored in this report are not limited to the Air Force but exist to varying degrees within the general population. That is, biases toward groups of people who are perceived to be different is a common challenge that affects virtually everyone.

Organization of This Report

The remainder of this report is organized as follows:

- Chapter 2 provides background on DoD and Air Force medical standards.
- Chapter 3 summarizes themes from our interviews with SMEs and stakeholders to identify potential benefits and barriers to implementing tailored standards.
- Chapter 4 describes the methods and results of a survey used to identify potential cultural barriers to tailored medical standards.
- Chapter 5 presents conclusions and study limitations.

We provide four appendixes with background information about the career fields, interview and survey materials, and additional details about the study approach and analyses. Appendix A provides examples of medical standards for the three Air Force specialty areas (i.e., cyber, aircraft maintenance, and RPA career fields) included in our SME discussions. Appendix B provides a copy of the SME discussion protocol. Appendix C provides one version of the survey used to explore airmen attitudes toward tailored standards. Appendix D provides additional details on how we analyzed the survey data and additional results not discussed in Chapter 4.

---

[3] According to personnel records, the Air Force had more than 20,000 airmen in cyber-related career fields in fiscal year 2018.

2. Overview of Department of Defense and Air Force Medical Standards

All applicants for military service undergo screening for age, citizenship, education, aptitude, physical and mental health, dependency status, and moral character. The health evaluation screens for potential medical disqualification across some 29 clinical (condition) categories. Among the medical characteristics that would result in disqualification are overweight or underweight, hearing loss, vision loss, and poor dentition.

DoD sets medical standards for applicants and service members already, but for Air Force applicants and airmen, the Air Force sets polices that provide additional guidance and specifications. Likewise, DoD sets standards for deployment and retention, which include medical readiness requirements, and the Air Force builds on those to set airmen deployment and retention standards. This chapter provides an overview of DoD and Air Force policies for medical standards. Because the policies and stakeholders involved in setting and implementing these standards are numerous and complex, we first provide context for key factors that can affect how medical standards are set and implemented before providing an overview of specific policies. Later in the chapter, we briefly outline how standards are applied at the individual level and then present our insights into how the numerous and layered policies create both flexibilities and barriers for the Air Force to tailor medical standards.

Overview of Key Factors for Military Medical Standards

To introduce how medical standards are used by the Air Force, we outline key factors relevant to setting and applying medical standards in the military. Those factors are the specificity of the standard, the timing in which the standard is applied in an airman's career, and the purpose of the standard (see Figure 2.1). We describe each of these factors in the following section.

Figure 2.1. Overview of Key Factors for Medical Standards in the Military

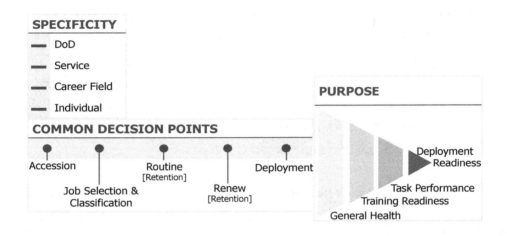

In Figure 2.1, the specificity of a medical standard reflects the population(s) affected by the standard. At the broadest level, DoD maintains policies relevant to all service members. For example, a history of asthma symptoms or treatment for asthma after one's 13th birthday is a disqualifying condition to serving in the military (DoDI 6130.03, 2018). Next, DoD components can have service-specific standards (e.g., Air Force use of abdominal circumference [AC] as a measure of body composition). The application of service-specific standards is followed by the application of standards for individual career fields or communities within a service, such as establishing airsickness as a disqualifier for pilots.[4] Ultimately, how a standard affects the qualifications of a particular individual to serve may need to be considered when weighing requests for a waiver,[5] which is an official exemption from policy (i.e., the individual is waived from meeting the particular medical standard set in policy).

The timing at which medical standards are applied across an airman's career is another important consideration. Common decision points include the following:

---

[4] According to the *USAF Medical Standards Directory (MSD)*, airsickness with medical evidence of organic or psychiatric pathology would disqualify Flying Class II and III (U.S. Air Force, 2018).

[5] A *medical waiver* is defined as

> A formal request to consider the suitability for service of an applicant who, because of current or past medical conditions, does not meet medical standards. Upon the completion of a thorough review, the applicant may be considered for a waiver. The applicant must have displayed sufficient mitigating circumstances/provided medical documentation that clearly justify waiver consideration. The Secretaries of the Military Departments may delegate the final approval authority for all waivers (DoDI 6130.03, 2018, pp. 47–48).

- accession (Should we allow this person to join the military?)
- job selection and classification (Should we allow this person to enter a particular career field?)
- routine (Should we allow this person to remain in the career field or Air Force?)
- renew (Should we allow this person to renew or extend a service contract?)
- deployment (Should we allow this person to deploy at this time to a certain location?).

Finally, DoD policy outlines the purposes for accession medical standards, which also inform medical standards applied at other common decision points, including deployment and retention. These purposes generally fall into four broad categories: (1) general health, (2) training readiness, (3) job-specific task performance, and (4) deployment readiness. Table 2.1 shows how the purposes of policy fall into these four broad categories.

Table 2.1. Primary Reasons for Department of Defense Medical Accession Standards

Purpose of Accession Medical Standard	Purpose Category
"(1) Free of contagious diseases that may endanger the health of other personnel."	General health
"(2) Free of medical conditions or physical defects that may reasonably be expected to require excessive time lost from duty for necessary treatment or hospitalization, or may result in separation from the Military Service for medical unfitness."	General health
"(3) Medically capable of satisfactorily completing required training and initial period of contracted service."	Training readiness
"(4) Medically capable of performing duties without aggravating existing physical defects or medical conditions."	Job-specific task performance
"(5) Medically adaptable to the military environment without geographical area limitations."	Deployment readiness

SOURCE: DoDI 6130.03, 2018, pp. 4–5.
NOTE: DoDI 6130.03 (2018, p. 4) also directs the services to "[u]se common medical standards for appointment, enlistment, or induction of personnel into the Military Services and eliminate inconsistencies and inequities in the DoD Components based on race, sex, or location of examination when applying these standards."

In the following sections, we outline how medical standards are most commonly applied to DoD and Air Force military personnel. We also include a brief discussion of relevant policies that need to be considered when evaluating the potential for tailoring medical standards in the Air Force.

How Medical Standards Are Applied to Individuals

At accession, applicants are screened for age, citizenship, education, aptitude, health, physical fitness, dependency status, and moral character. The medical assessment consists of a clinical exam, lab tests, hearing and vision evaluations, and physical measurements to screen for

29 categories of potential disqualifiers (e.g., heart, urinary system, spine and sacroiliac joint conditions, upper and lower extremity conditions).

For enlisted personnel, medical assessments are conducted by medical providers at Military Entrance Processing Station (MEPS) and, for officer personnel, assessments are conducted through DoD Medical Examination Review Board.[6]

Job selection and classification—the Air Force's selection of applicants for jobs—involves aligning occupation-specific requirements with personnel qualifications. Job selection for enlisted personnel can occur during accession while processing applicants at MEPS, after accession at basic military training (BMT), or during post-BMT training (U.S. Military Entrance Processing Command, 2017). Officer job selection occurs after accession and completion of the requirements to become an officer. Similar to the accession process, personnel qualifications at job selection include meeting medical and physical standards, satisfying criteria for aptitude, and completing job-specific trainings.

Retention standards define the requirements that must be met to remain a military member. These standards may be applied at regular intervals (e.g., annually) or may be applied when renewing or extending a contract, or both. DoD outlines baseline medical and physical retention standards, and the Air Force tailors these to meet requirements of each AFSC (or job description), based, in part, on the AFSC's accession standards.

Deployment standards stipulate requirements for "any temporary duty [TDY] where Contingency, Exercise, and Deployment TDY orders were issued, and the TDY location is outside of the United States" (AFI 48-123, 2018, p. 67). Some service members may be able to meet retention standards but not meet standards for deployment. For example, a person with a temporary medical condition or a person who does not pass a Physical Fitness Test (PFT) may be temporarily nondeployable. According to Air Force policy, those who fail to meet the medical and physical deployability and retention standards for more than one year either receive an administrative separation per AFI 36-3208 (2018) or may be eligible for disability benefits as described in AFI 36-3212 (2009). In February 2018, the Office of the Under Secretary of Defense for Personnel and Readiness (OSD P&R) provided interim policy guidance on retention of nondeployable service members indicating the following:

> [S]ervice members who have been non-deployable for more than 12 consecutive months, for any reason, will be processed for administrative separation in accordance with Department of Defense Instruction (DoDI) 1332.14, Enlisted Administrative Separations, or DoD Instruction 1332.30, Separation of Regular and Reserve Commissioned Officers, or will be referred into the Disability

---

[6] Although the medical screening processes at accession do not vary much by accession source, the time frames over which medical issues manifest and can be addressed vary by accession source. For enlisted applicants, all attend BMT but follow-on initial skills training varies by Air Force specialty. This initial skills training (known as *technical training* in the Air Force) can range from weeks to months. For officer applicants, time spent in accession programs range from weeks to years. For example, Air Force Academy cadets spend years preparing for commission versus the weeks or months spent by those who attend Officer Training School.

Evaluation System in accordance with DoDI 1332.18, Disability Evaluation System (DES) (Wilkie, 2018).

Insights on Potential Policy Flexibilities and Barriers That Could Affect Tailoring Medical Standards

Numerous policy documents detail the medical standards that span the range of specificity levels and decision points. In this section and Table 2.2, we present the principal documents that guide DoD, Air Force, and combatant command (COCOM) policies as they apply to both officer and enlisted applicants and personnel.

Table 2.2. Key Policy Documents Guiding Medical and Physical Standards

Topic Addressed	Policy	Title	Date
Applicants' medical conditions and physical fitness	DoDI 6130.03	*Medical Standards for Appointment, Enlistment, or Induction in the Military Services*	May 6, 2018
	AFI 48-123*	*Medical Examinations and Standards*	January 28, 2018
Applicants' physical fitness	DoDD 1308.1	*Physical Fitness and Body Fat Program*	June 30, 2004
	DoDI 1308.3	*Physical Fitness and Body Fat Programs Procedures*	November 5, 2002
	AFI 36-2905	*Fitness Program*	August 27, 2015
Flying classes, special operational duty, and retention	MSD	*USAF Medical Standards Directory (MSD)*	May 24, 2018
Personnel requirements and qualifications required for each AFSC	AFECD	*Air Force Enlisted Classification Directory (AFECD)*	October 31, 2017
	AFOCD	*Air Force Officer Classification Directory (AFOCD)*	October 31, 2017
Deployment-specific medical and physical standards in each of the ten COCOM regions	DoDI 6490.07	*Deployment-Limiting Medical Conditions for Service Members and DoD Civilian Employees*	February 5, 2010
	COCOM	COCOM Reporting Instructions**	[multiple]
Retention criteria for nondeployable personnel	DoD memorandum*	DoD Retention Policy for Nondeployable Service Members	February 14, 2018

SOURCES: Each policy is listed in this report's bibliography.
NOTES: AFI 48-123 has been modified in recent years; the most recent version is dated January 28, 2018.
DoDD = Department of Defense Directive.
* See Wilkie, 2018.
** Using SME discussions, each COCOM may have additional medical and physical standards associated with specific deployment requirements.

Taken together, these policies highlight several overarching points: (1) DoD and Air Force have their own policy guidance, but DoD policy informs Air Force policy; (2) the services can waive various conditions at accession but these waiver policies are not tailored to specific occupations; (3) service-specific medical standards are applied when more stringent requirements are needed for specific occupations (e.g., aircraft pilots); (4) retention standards and decisions are dependent on deployment standards and deployability, which is specifically emphasized in recent policy guidance from DoD; and, (5) individuals not meeting deployment standards can be retained but limited capabilities must be documented (e.g., assignment limitation code). These points suggest that the each service, including the Air Force, has some flexibility in determining medical standards,[7] through the waiver process at accessions and use of assignment limitation codes for retention and deployability (Krull et al., 2019). Nonetheless, use of these authorities may conflict with broader DoD goals and directives for all military personnel to be worldwide deployable.

---

[7] For example, 577 recruits applied for a waiver for a vision-related disorder (refraction and accommodation) in 2015. Of those, 378 were approved. (Boivin et al., 2016).

3. Stakeholder and Subject-Matter Expert Perceptions of Tailoring Standards

To understand the potential costs and benefits of tailored medical and physical standards, we conducted semistructured interviews with 11 SMEs across the following organizations: Air Education and Training Command (AETC), Air Force Recruiting Service (AFRS), Accessions and Training Division within Headquarters Air Force Military Force Management Policy (AF/A1PT), Air National Guard (ANG), Military Personnel Policy (MPP) within OSD P&R, and the Accession Medical Standards Working Group (AMSWG). SMEs consisted of officers (O-5 and higher), enlisted (E-7 and higher), and civilians in leadership positions (e.g., branch chiefs and assistant directors). In general, these discussions were held with only one SME from each organization.

We also held seven discussions with a total of 14 individuals affiliated with career fields involving cyber, aircraft maintenance, and RPA. The majority of these SMEs were career field managers.

Discussions addressed two key questions related to tailoring medical and physical standards. First, SMEs were asked about the value, if any, to tailoring medical and/or physical standards in the Air Force (Appendix B). Depending on how SMEs responded, we used one or more prompts to determine whether the perceived value differed by component (e.g., active, ANG, Reserve), career field (e.g., cyber, personnel, aircraft maintenance), or specific medical or physical condition (e.g., asthma, hearing impairment, depression). Next, we asked SMEs about the major barriers to implementing tailored medical and/or physical standards in the Air Force. Follow-up prompts addressed the challenges with implementing tailored standards for only a subset of specialties, accommodations that may be needed, the level of anticipated leadership support, and policies that would need to change.

Some discussions also addressed opportunities and challenges that the Air Force might face in using alternative tests to support decisions for screening applicants. More specifically, the aim of these questions was to get a more general sense of attitudes toward genetic testing as an example of alternative tests and what type of policies would be supported. For policy-oriented discussions, these topics were applied to DoD and Air Force policies; for career field discussions, topics were applied to the career fields with which individuals were most familiar. For the career field discussions, participants were affiliated with career fields involving cyber, aircraft maintenance, and RPA. We selected these three career fields to represent a range of cognitive and physical requirements.

Interview Results and Themes

The next sections highlight the major themes from our analysis of the interview notes. To analyze discussions, notes were uploaded to Dedoose, a research tool for qualitative and mixed methods data analysis. Discussions were first coded by the primary topic areas addressed in researcher-posed questions. Then, subcodes were developed based on themes that arose from discussants' comments. One RAND researcher coded the discussions. The project leaders reviewed the application of these codes and resulting themes to ensure standardization. It is important to note that the themes and direct quotes represent the perceptions of these SMEs in our sample and may not reflect the general perceptions of other airmen.

In General, Interview Participants Questioned the Value of Tailoring Medical Standards

When discussing tailoring standards, two individuals provided positive comments. For example, one Air Force cyber professional stated, "How do we get and retain talent? If a guy has a missing leg but can hack, I don't care. I'll take him, same with asthma or sleep apnea." Overall, however, discussants provided more negative than positive comments about the impacts of tailored standards.

Cultural Considerations

In discussing potential issues with tailoring standards for particular career fields, several SMEs discussed cultural considerations. For example, one individual in a cyber career field commented on others' reactions to those in cyber being allowed to enter or stay in the Air Force based on physical standards that were different from those applied to other career fields. He noted, "The question is, 'If we let cyber not take PT [physical training] and they look different, how will others react when they see them?'"

Relatedly, one person also commented on the implications that changing physical standards might have on perceptions of leadership. He addressed potential implications of individuals becoming commanders who could enter and stay in the Air Force based on standards that differed from those applied to the individuals they lead. He noted, "It's hard to have a commander who doesn't meet requirements but expects others to meet requirements. How would airmen respond to a commander who doesn't meet Air Force standards but is trying to enforce them for others?"

Given these cultural challenges, some individuals suggested that new civil service jobs could be created as a potentially acceptable solution to filling skill gaps rather than tailoring medical and physical standards for military personnel.

Deployment Considerations

Individuals also emphasized the perceived utility of maintaining current medical and physical standards to address deployment needs. For example, several noted the perceived importance of most, if not all, airmen being able to deploy. Among active-duty personnel, discussants indicated that this requirement ensures those in certain career fields are not overly burdened during deployments. One individual commented:

> I've sent many coms [communications] airmen overseas, but even though their job was coms, they still had to be able to work a guard post . . . If you shrink the pool on either side for people who can take these assignments, it will stretch the rest of the force out.

One individual perceived that the components, such as ANG and Reserve, should also maintain current physical and medical standards. He believed this ensures that the components can better support the active-duty force. He stated, "I don't think it's a good idea to change the component standards, since we all support the active duty. We need to support and back fill active people, so different standards would not be in our interests."

Impact on Recruitment

Some believed that tailored standards were unnecessary because they did not perceive issues in recruiting individuals into career fields. One Air Force cyber professional commented, "We are looking for a small number of people [who] are looking to serve, and I don't think we are going to be losing people based on standards." Another Air Force maintenance professional stated, "In the past few years, we've been able to close our bathtub of inventory [i.e., limited number of personnel] quickly. We've had great success in bringing airmen into maintenance AFSCs. As a whole, we retain as good as other AFSCs."

In addition, discussants also noted that waivers for different medical conditions can currently be issued on a case-by-case basis, if needed. They believed that this allows exceptional individuals to join, even if they do not meet all current standards. Therefore, again, they did not perceive a need to tailor standards. Addressing this factor, one discussant noted, "AFRS is very open to reviewing any and all medical standards that may prohibit qualified airmen from serving." Similarly, another discussant stated, "We do risk analysis to the Air Force. . . . Generally, these people [who receive waivers] are exceptional, like an MIT grad with asthma. They'll go through the medical waiver."

Several discussants also addressed the difficulty in estimating the potential impact of changing standards on improving future Air Force recruitment. Many individuals might not apply to join the Air Force because they know they do not meet current medical standards. In addition, many who express interest in the joining the Air Force might be disqualified without documentation for the disqualification reason. One discussant involved in Air Force recruiting stated, "If [a potential recruit] is overweight, then it doesn't get documented. [We] get rid of 80 to 90 percent [of those who are overweight] before the process even starts." These factors hinder analysts' ability to create detailed prediction models involving recruitment impacts following modified medical and physical standards.

Interviews Provided Mixed Feedback on Use of Genetic Testing

Only three individuals discussed the topic of genetic testing as part of the Air Force screening process. Feedback regarding these tests were mixed. Discussing the positive aspects of genetic testing, one discussant stated:

> When you join the military, you give up a lot of rights. Shoot, we have to take HIV tests. What other companies ask you to do that? The U.S. Air Force is the most forward-thinking and tech-based service, in my opinion, so if we were able to sell this [genetic testing information] with the member, [the Air Force] could sell it as a positive. Money may be an issue, but there are not many people that are uber privacy people in the military.

However, another person commented:

> When we started doing DNA testing, or the anthrax vaccine route, there wasn't a lot of trust in that and we lost a lot of good people who got out of the service rather than going through the vaccine process. So, we may lose people who decide not to serve since decisions won't be made on effort or performance but on genetic conditions.

Given the small size of the interview sample, findings are meant to illustrate potential themes rather than generalize findings to other Air Force personnel. Nonetheless, privacy and trust were identified as important factors to consider when using genetic testing as indicated in interviews and further supported by survey findings (discussed in Chapter 4).

Summary

Interview participants identified a culture not accepting of airmen who do not meet standards and airmen not being able to meet deployment medical standards as potential barriers. Some interviewees also noted that tailored medical standards were not needed, that the Air Force can recruit enough individuals with the current system of medical standards and individual waivers. Finally, only three participants discussed genetic testing. Feedback on genetic testing was mixed but points to privacy and trust as factors that the Air Force should consider if it plans to use genetic testing to inform certain decisions about applicants.

4. Survey of Cultural Barriers to Tailoring Medical Standards

As highlighted through our interviews with SMEs, the Air Force will need to address a variety of perceived barriers to successfully implement tailored medical or physical standards. Any change initiative will require some level of buy-in regardless of the justification and planning involved to implement the change. To understand how cultural barriers could affect the acceptance of tailoring medical standards, we developed and fielded a survey with airmen. In this chapter, we describe the survey content, methodology, and results.

Survey Content and Administration

The survey was designed to address three general questions:[8]

- Are airmen's attitudes toward coworkers affected by those coworkers' medical conditions?
- Do airmen perceive that coworkers who do not meet certain standards will affect the coworkers' performance and safety of others?
- How do airmen feel about various policy options for use of medical accession or other standards?

We drew from relevant literature and constructed our survey assessing several established attitudes and belief patterns that previously have shown to affect the acceptance of individuals in the workplace (further detail on the sources for our constructs and measures can be found in Appendixes C and D). Each survey packet contained a vignette and set of survey items that focused on one of two standards, specifically Air Force **weight** standards[9] or Air Force **hearing** standards. Each participant was randomly assigned to a survey condition, so half received questions on weight standards ($n = 280$) and half on hearing standards ($n = 279$). We focused on weight and hearing issues partly because they disqualify large numbers of individuals from joining the military (Boivin et al., 2016). In addition, symptoms associated with these issues tend to differ (e.g., visibility of issue), thereby facilitating assessment of differences in perceptions across varied health issues.

Survey Structure

The first page of the survey packet contained an informed consent form, which provided information regarding the project sponsor (the RAND Corporation) and the study's purpose. In

---

[8] A copy of the survey is provided in Appendix C.

[9] We chose the term *weight standards* as a simpler way of characterizing the fictional airman (Thompson), and these weight standards also directly tie back to weight and height standards used for accession. It is important to note, however, that the Air Force uses AC to measure body composition for its regular fitness assessments.

addition, participants were informed that their participation was voluntary and that the survey would take approximately 20 minutes to complete. They were also assured anonymity. Notably, participants completed the paper-based survey in person, with other participants and researchers present. In this context, participants might have been reluctant to provide accurate information about their own attitudes and knowledge regarding the issues addressed.

In the first section of the survey, participants received a vignette that included a description of another airman. The status and career field of the airman were designed to correspond with each participant's characteristics. Specifically, among participants who were enlisted personnel, the airman was described as an airman Basic (E1) in participants' career field. Among those who were officers, the individual was described as an Air Force 2nd Lieutenant (O1) in participants' career field. In addition, the airman was described as not meeting one of the current requirements to join the Air Force, either the weight standard or the hearing standard. As described previously, participants were randomly assigned to receive a vignette and survey items that focused on either Air Force weight standards or Air Force hearing standards. The provided vignettes are listed in Table 4.1.

Table 4.1. Experimentally Manipulated Vignettes

Weight Condition	Hearing Condition
In this section, please imagine that an [Air Force 2nd lieutenant (O1)/Airman Basic (E1)] in your career field, named Thompson, has been assigned to your unit. When he joined the Air Force, Thompson's weight was over the current Air Force body fat standards, so he is considered overweight. He met all other current requirements to join the Air Force. Thompson's weight has stayed about the same since he joined. He meets all other current Air Force standards. Thompson is able to perform all essential job duties. However, Thompson is not eligible to deploy to some locations because he does not meet the body fat standards for those deployed locations.	In this section, please imagine that an [Air Force 2nd lieutenant (O1)/Airman Basic (E1)] in your career field, named Thompson, has been assigned to your unit. When he joined the Air Force, Thompson's hearing was below the current Air Force hearing standards—partial hearing. He met all other current requirements to join the Air Force. Thompson's hearing has stayed about the same since he joined. He meets all other current Air Force standards. Thompson is able to perform all essential job duties. However, Thompson is not eligible to deploy to some locations because he does not meet the hearing standards for those deployed locations.

The subsequent sections on the survey organized questions by broad topic areas, so the survey design provides a framework for the areas of interest that we addressed (Table 4.2). In the second section, we addressed behavioral inclinations toward and perceptions of airmen with different health issues. Several items in this section specifically focused on those who either do not meet Air Force weight standards or do not meet Air Force hearing standards, again depending on survey condition. In the third section, we examined participants' experience with working with others who have had either weight issues or hearing issues, based on the survey condition to which each participant was assigned. In the fourth section, we assessed participants' perceptions of genetic testing. All participants received the same genetic testing questions. In the final survey section, we asked demographic questions of all participants.[10]

Table 4.2. Cultural Perceptions: Attitude and Behavior Measures Included on the Survey with Example Items

Scale Name	Example Item	Alpha*
Candidate Employability	Quality of performance on core job tasks Potential for promotion	.87
Other Work Evaluations	Ability to handle several tasks at once Ability to handle challenging job assignments	.96
Stigma	Thompson's hearing . . . will put coworkers at risk. Thompson's weight . . . will cause problems with coworker relations.	.87
Discriminatory Judgments	Thompson should NOT be promoted over other Air Force members of similar performance quality who meet the standards. The Air Force should avoid hiring people with Thompson's [condition], unless Thompson has higher than average technical skills.	.78
Expectancies	I believe that airmen with [condition] issues slow down the rate at which work is completed.	.85
Unfairness of Deployment Accommodations	How would you feel about Thompson not deploying? . . . unfair . . . undeserved	.89
Behaviors: Facilitation	Active-duty personnel in the Air Force would . . . help airmen with [condition] issues.	.86
Behaviors: Harm	Active-duty personnel in the Air Force would . . . harass airmen with [condition] issues.	.84

NOTE: * = Alpha is an index for the internal consistency of a measure and is a function of the interrelatedness among items and number of items in a measure. Alpha can range between 0 and 1, with values above .7 generally considered acceptable as a rule of thumb for measures with relatively few items (See Cortina [1993] for a critical examination of alpha).

Survey Administration

The survey was administered over the course of two days at Keesler Air Force Base in Biloxi, Mississippi, to airmen and officers in cyber-related career field training. Seven classes participated, made up of 575 airmen in total. Participation was voluntary, and some airmen did

---

[10] Before administering the survey to large groups of participants, we conducted cognitive interviews with four Air Force officers, who each held a rank lower than O4 (Major). These interviews addressed several topics, including item and response option interpretation, clarity of items and instructions, and recall. We modified survey content based on the feedback we received.

not participate: 11 left all of the survey blank and an additional five left more than 50 percent of the items missing. After removing these airmen from the sample, 559 participants remained.

The majority (66 percent) of participants were enlisted, ranging from E-1 (13 percent) to senior NCOs of E-6 and above (11 percent). The officers (34 percent) also ranged somewhat, although the majority were second lieutenants (26 percent), while the remainder were higher ranks. About 5 percent did not report their paygrades. Sixty-two percent identified themselves as non-Hispanic white; the majority (87 percent) were male. Reported AFSCs included Cyber Officer (17XX, 33 percent), Cyber Warfare Operations (1B4X1, 18 percent), Cyber Transport Systems (3D1X2, 17 percent), Radio Frequency Transmission Systems (3D1X3, 10 percent), Cyber Systems Operations (3D0X2, 7 percent), Client Systems (3D1X1, 5 percent), and Other (8 percent).[11]

Survey Analysis and Findings

Our questions centered on the acceptance and potential barriers to acceptance of various medical standards and what the Air Force might wish to consider should they decide to modify medical standards. To answer our questions, we first examined simple comparisons to determine whether airmen differed in their perceptions along the variety of relevant dimensions shown in Table 4.2. Knowledge of group differences among airmen's perceptions would facilitate further exploration of concerns among particular communities and might help hone messaging required during implementation. Thus, we were interested in going beyond medical and physical conditions (in our case, examination of attitudes regarding hearing and weight standards) to include other factors, such as tenure and cyber-relatedness of career field, to determine whether these factors were related to how accepting airmen were of people who did not meet standards. We examined condition (hearing versus weight) and a set of potentially relevant service history characteristics as follows:

- commissioning status (enlisted versus officer)
- approximate tenure (E-1-E-4 and O1-O2 versus E-5+ and O-3+)
- cyber orientation of career field (17XX, AB4X1, 3D0X1, 3D0X2, 3D0X3, and 3D0X4 versus 3D1X1, 3D1X2, and 3D1X3).

Survey Responses Did Not Consistently Vary Across Service History Characteristics

In general, few constructs differed between airmen in more and less cyber-oriented career fields ($ps > .05$). There was a significant difference in perceived unfairness of deployment accommodations such that airmen in more cyber-related career fields considered accommodations on average less fair ($\overline{x} = 3.4$ for cyber-related career fields, $\overline{x} = 3.1$ for less technical career fields; $t(528) = -3.5, p < .05$). As these constructs were scored on 5-point scales,

---

[11] Because of rounding, percentages do not add up to 100.

a score of 3 corresponded with the neutral or midpoint option; by this measure, airmen were close to that neutral midpoint of perceptions of unfairness of accommodations regardless of what their career field was. Similarly, very few differences between officers and enlisted respondents were significant. The exception was for behaviors related to harm—enlisted personnel were significantly more likely than officers to affirm that personnel would behave in a manner that might harm Thompson; although, in both groups, the average score indicated that such behaviors would occur "somewhat infrequently" ($\bar{x}$ = 2.4 enlisted, $\bar{x}$ = 2.0 officer; $t(553) = 4.57, p < .05$).

Several dimensions did vary based on approximate tenure or time in the Air Force. More junior personnel were more likely to endorse discriminatory judgments and have more negative expectancies of Thompson. However, more senior personnel were more likely to indicate that deployment accommodations were unfair and more likely to affirm that personnel would behave in a manner that might harm Thompson. Mean differences are displayed in Table 4.3, along with relevant statistics.

Table 4.3. Significant Differences on Cultural Perceptions by Approximate Tenure: Attitude and Behavior Measures

Scale Name	E-1-E-4 and O1-O2 Mean	E-5+ and O-3+ Mean	t-test, p < .05
Discriminatory Judgments	2.81	2.63	$t(527) = 2.45$
Expectancies	2.32	2.13	$t(530) = 2.46$
Unfairness of Deployment Accommodations	3.22	3.43	$t(522) = -2.23$
Behaviors: Harm	2.20	2.46	$t(528) = -3.17$

Perceptions About Airman Not Meeting Hearing and Weight Standards Generally Negative but Vary by Condition

Our first step was to take these dimensions along which airmen can differ and determine whether groups were different (i.e., we looked for main effects with a series of independent samples t-tests). Although some service history factors were relevant for some types of outcomes, the most consistent pattern by far was found for condition. On a variety of measures, attitudes about Thompson as a coworker were affected by whether Thompson failed to meet weight or hearing standards. On average, participants in the weight condition had less-positive views of Thompson than did those in the hearing condition on every dimension considered.

For example, responses favored the hearing condition related to potential exemptions from deployment, which might be considered a type of accommodation for those who did not meet current standards. More specifically, to address perceptions regarding this type of policy, we asked participants how they would feel about Thompson not deploying while others in their unit deploy. We presented participants with six pairs of adjectives that have been used previously to assess perceived fairness of accommodations for certain individuals (McLaughlin, Bell, and Stringer, 2004). Participants responded to using a 5-point rating scale for each pair: fair-unfair; necessary-unnecessary; reasonable-unreasonable; positive-negative; just-unjust; and deserved-undeserved.[12] Responses indicated that a deployment exemption would be more reasonable for an airman with a hearing condition. Figure 4.1 provides the specific responses, separated by the weight and hearing conditions.

Figure 4.1. Feelings About Thompson Not Deploying, by Hearing and Weight Survey Condition

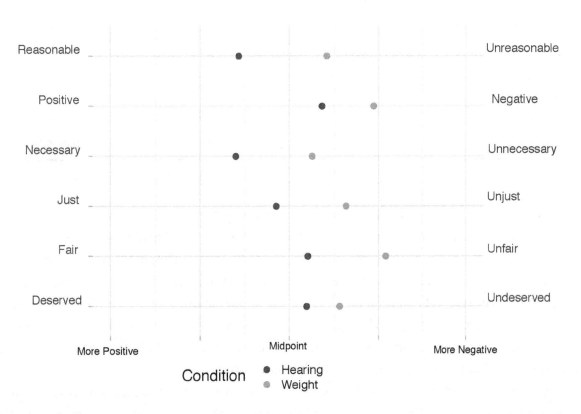

On average, participants in the weight condition also had less-positive views of Thompson than did those in the hearing condition in terms of employability and expectations of Thompson's performance. Mean differences are displayed in Table 4.4. Employability and other work evaluations were less positive, such that respondents were less likely to think that Thompson's quality of performance would be as high, on average, if Thompson was overweight rather than if Thompson had not met hearing standards. Respondents were more likely to endorse

---

[12] Coefficient alpha for this scale was acceptable at $\alpha = .89$.

various stigma-related beliefs, on average; endorsed more discriminatory judgments, had higher negative expectancies, saw accommodations as less fair, and predicted that other airmen would be less helpful and more harmful in their behavior, on average, when Thompson did not meet standards of weight rather than hearing.

Table 4.4. Significant Differences on Cultural Perceptions by Hearing and Weight Standards: Attitude and Behavior Measures

Scale Name	Hearing Mean	Weight Mean	t-test, $p < .05$
Candidate Employability	3.44	3.07	$t(541) = 7.83$
Other Work Evaluations	3.52	3.03	$t(538) = 7.83$
Stigma	2.21	2.68	$t(556) = -8.34$
Discriminatory Judgments	2.63	2.89	$t(552) = -3.8$
Expectancies	2.04	2.48	$t(555) = -6.71$
Unfairness of Deployment Accommodations	2.91	3.65	$t(547) = -9.58$
Behaviors: Facilitation	3.98	3.85	$t(553) = 2.09$
Behaviors: Harm	2.12	2.42	$t(553) = -4.14$

Although these results were generally consistent across topic areas (i.e., scales) on the survey, we also examined individual items within these scales to determine if we could discern nuance in how Thompson was perceived (Appendix D). For each condition, we standardized items so we could compare consistently across them and sorted them by positivity of score. Specifically, overweight Thompson fared worse on items relating to self-discipline and setting a good example. Also, overweight Thompson was seen as having more control over his weight. In contrast, Thompson not meeting the hearing standards was more likely to generate concerns that he would be difficult to work with and might put coworkers at risk.

We also asked participants in both conditions to indicate whether airmen with a variety of medical conditions would be able to accomplish the work of the Air Force. Interestingly, by this assessment, both weight and hearing conditions were viewed relatively positively, with substantial majorities of respondents indicating that an overweight (77 percent) airmen and an airman with a hearing impairment (70 percent) *could* perform essential job tasks. This is in marked contrast to other conditions that were seen as very problematic in terms of job execution. For example, relatively few participants thought airmen with a prescription drug addiction (18 percent) or an alcohol addiction (24 percent) could do the job, as can be seen in Figure 4.2.

Figure 4.2. Perceptions Regarding Whether Airmen with Various Medical Conditions Could Perform Air Force Job

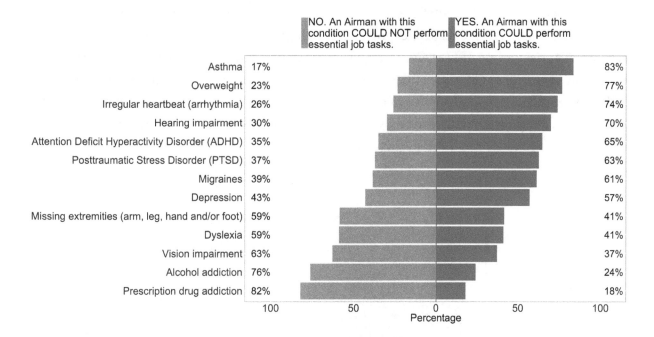

Therefore, although preferences were clear for a hearing-impaired airman—and an airman not meeting weight standard was considered less preferable—there was nuance to these attitudes. In particular, a hearing impairment was more associated with potential safety risks and difficulty making accommodations, and a weight impairment was more likely to be seen as a matter of poor personal discipline. However, in both cases, airmen who did not meet these standards were likely to be able to do their jobs.

Quality of Interactions Can Influence Attitudes

We also explored whether these effects on various attitudes and preferences were still found when a condition and the service history factors (e.g., commissioning status, approximate tenure, cyber-relatedness of career field) were all entered into the same model. Moreover, we wanted to consider whether other aspects of experience might temper these negative effects. Specifically, previous research suggests that multiple, high-quality interactions with those in another group, such as those with certain conditions, can reduce prejudice and discrimination toward that group (e.g., Pettigrew and Tropp, 2006; Turner et al., 2008). Thus, for each of our relevant outcomes, we examined models with the same set of predictors: respondents' own weight and hearing condition status (self-status), condition, service history characteristics, and the extensiveness and quality of experience with coworkers and others with Thompson's condition. All variables except extent and quality of experience were entered first; then, extent and quality were added as a second block so that we could determine whether these factors accounted for significant additional variance, controlling for all other variables already in the model.

In general, as shown in Table 4.5, a condition was associated with each outcome, controlling for all other predictors. As shown upon examination of main effects, the weight condition was associated with less-positive attitudes. In some cases, other predictors also made a significant contribution, such as cyber-relatedness of career field (more cyber-related career fields saw accommodation as more unfair) and commissioning status (enlisted personnel were more likely to indicate greater harm behavior frequency). When experience and quality of interaction were added to the models, in the majority of cases these factors also significantly improved the model, and the effect was consistently driven by quality of interaction such that higher-quality interactions were related to more-positive attitudes.

Table 4.5. Summary Results of Regression Models Examining Associating Condition and Service History Characteristics and Experience and Quality of Interaction with Cultural Perceptions

Model	Predictors	Standardized Coefficients for Each Outcome						
		Candidate Employability	Other Work Evaluations	Discriminatory Judgments	Stigma	Behaviors: Harm	Behaviors: Facilitation	Unfairness of Deployment Accommodations
1	Self-status (hearing)	.021	-.015	-.040	.000	.002	-.066	-.067
	Self-status (weight)	-.013	-.018	-.083	-.070	.010	.017	.075
	Tenure	.063	.046	-.084	-.037	.072	.000	.020
	Cyber-relatedness	.006	-.004	-.008	-.009	.044	-.020	.173
	Rank	-.029	-.033	.035	-.018	-.183**	.050	-.049
	Condition	-.343**	-.360**	.195**	.380**	.142**	-.093	.382**
R²		.126**	.122**	.058**	.148**	.059**	.015	.193**
2	Self-status (hearing)	.019	-.016	-.041	.002	.004	-.069	-.066
	Self-status (weight)	-.055	-.058	-.036	-.026	.033	-.012	.079
	Tenure	.055	.039	-.061	-.025	.074	-.003	.016
	Cyber-relatedness	-.009	-.017	.000	.004	.053	-.030	.177
	Rank	-.044	-.048	.057	.001	-.174**	.039	-.048
	Condition	-.360**	-.378*	.256	.400**	.138**	-.092	.368**
	Extent of interactions	.038	.042	-.121*	-.049	-.001	.007	.024
	Quality of interactions	.313**	.296**	-.311**	-.339**	-.201	.238**	-.049
R²		.226**	.209**	.170**	.266**	.099**	.070**	.195**

NOTE: * = $p < .05$; ** = $p < .001$.

23

Majority Not Supportive of Using Genetic Testing

In addition to policy options to tailor standards, the Air Force might consider new tools and technologies for screening and classifying airmen into job specialties. One policy option that the Air Force might review involves use of genetic tests to support these types of decisions. Among the many factors that would need to be considered prior to implementation of genetic screening (e.g., current laws, policies, privacy, test validity[13]) is the acceptability among those being screened (Rothstein, Roberts, and Guidotti, 2015).

There are multiple ways that the Air Force might consider using genetic testing. To address this question, we presented participants with seven possible uses of genetic test results and asked how they would feel about the Air Force using individuals' genetic test results for each (e.g., "to provide Air Force applicants with career guidance"). Participants indicated whether they opposed or supported each option for use of these results (1 = Oppose. I would oppose the Air Force using genetic testing for this purpose; 2 = Support. I would support the Air Force using genetic testing for this purpose).

The results indicated clear majorities responding that they did not support many policy applications of genetic testing, as shown in Table 4.6.

Table 4.6. Support for Various Policy Applications of Genetic Testing

Purpose of Genetic Test	Percentage Supporting
To prevent people entering the Air Force from joining certain Air Force specialties	25%
To assign people entering the Air Force into certain Air Force specialties	25%
To determine how often airmen should receive physical fitness assessments	28%
To screen out Air Force applicants at risk for behavioral disorders	38%
To screen out Air Force applicants at risk for physical conditions	44%
To provide Air Force applicants with career guidance	46%
To inform Air Force applicants of possible genetic disorders	80%

---

[13] For a broader discussion of genetic testing in the military, see De Castro et al. (2016) and Baruch and Hudson (2008).

Summary

The survey was designed to primarily answer three questions about airmen's attitudes toward medical standards:

- Are airmen's attitudes toward a coworker affected by those coworkers' medical or physical conditions?

  - Yes: In general, there were more positive perceptions of an airmen who did not meet hearing rather than weight standards.

- Do airmen perceive that coworkers who do not meet certain standards would affect performance and safety?

  - Yes: Although respondents indicated some safety concerns related to working with an airmen with a hearing condition, respondents in general felt that airmen not meeting either hearing or weight standards would be able to do the job.

- How do airmen feel about various policy options for use of medical accession or other standards?

  - In general, airmen indicated mixed support for the Air Force to use genetic testing, but the level of support varied depending on the purpose.

5. Conclusions and Options to Consider for Tailoring Medical Standards

In this chapter, we summarize major findings from the project and provide options for the Air Force to consider if it plans to tailor medical standards in the future.

Major Findings

Department of Defense Policies on Medical Standards May Present Policy Barriers to Air Force–Tailored Medical Standards

Although the Air Force can add more-stringent medical standards on top of DoD's medical standards and can waive certain conditions at accession, the first application of medical standards to Air Force applicants is by DoD. Also, a DoD memorandum on worldwide deployment requirements (DoDI, 2018) limits the extent to which the Air Force could have airmen not meet certain medical standards even if they could complete their core occupational tasks.

Subject-Matter Expert Discussions and Surveys of Cyber Airmen Reveal Potential Air Force Cultural Barriers to Tailoring Medical Standards

Our discussions with SMEs identified deployability requirements as a significant barrier to tailoring medical standards given that accessions and retention medical standards ultimately need to tie back to medical readiness to deploy. Some SMEs suggested that if deployability and meeting medical standards were not requirements, the Air Force should consider using civilians to meet critical skill gaps.

In general, SMEs from the career fields we examined (cyber, maintenance, and RPA) did not see a need to tailor medical standards. They were concerned about negative perceptions of airmen in their career fields were medical standards relaxed for their career fields. They also felt that recruiting and retention were sufficient under the current standards and that the waiver process offered enough flexibility to tailor standards to individual cases.

The survey findings suggest that relaxing medical standards may not be equally accepted by all airmen. For participants in the overweight survey condition, the top concerns about an overweight coworker related to perceptions of fairness and stereotypes: inability to set a good example and maintain self-discipline; unfair if accommodations provided (i.e., not required to deploy when other airmen in the career field would be required to deploy); and perceptions that airmen have control over their weight and, therefore, should be able to lose weight if so desired. In contrast, participants in the hearing impairment survey condition had concerns about performance and safety if they were to work alongside someone with a hearing impairment.

Although our policy review reveals that the Air Force collects biomarker data for limited purposes, the survey results indicate that airmen were not fully supportive of the use of one type of biomarker assessment—genetic testing—for purposes outside communicating potential genetic conditions. For example, survey responses indicated mixed support for use of genetic testing to screen and assign airmen to specific occupations.

Although our survey findings and discussions with SMEs are limited to a small group of individuals, they suggest that caution is needed when implementing tailored medical standards. To the extent cultural barriers are present, lowering standards may result in lower acceptance of coworkers. Acceptance of coworkers is an important aspect of workplace socialization and subsequent attitudinal commitment to an organization (Dodd-McCue and Wright, 1996; Saks and Ashforth, 1997). Therefore, the Air Force should evaluate attitudes and opinions regarding changing specific standards and how individuals may be affected by changing these standards. To increase acceptance, the Air Force would need to demonstrate that tailored standards do not affect the individual's performance or others' safety. Furthermore, acceptance could be further improved by ensuring that supervisors and commanders communicate the goals and importance of tailored standards and are held accountable for effectively implementing tailored standards.

Options for Approaches to Tailoring Medical Standards

Our findings identify opportunities and potential challenges with tailoring medical standards. Given the focus on cyber career fields and complexities of implementing any new standards, we offer options, not recommendations, for the Air Force to consider if it were to tailor medical standards to career field needs.

Consider Voluntary and Limited Trial Programs for Nondecisional Biomarker Applications

The survey findings indicate that few airmen would be fully supportive of the Air Force using genetic information to make administrative decisions, such as whether someone could be denied entry into the Air Force or what career field they would enter. However, a majority (80 percent) of participants supported the idea of the Air Force informing applicants of a possible genetic disorder. Using these findings, the Air Force should tread carefully with plans to further implement biomarkers into the accession process. If new biomarker technologies were to be used, the Air Force should first consider a voluntary program on a trial basis that would use results to inform applicants of health risks (or benefits) but not use the information to make selection, classification, or other personnel decisions.

Address Potential Concerns of Fairness Before Tailoring Medical Standards

Understanding the underlying source of any concern is an important step in developing a strategy to address cultural barriers to tailoring standards. The survey results and SME feedback in this study indicated that cultural barriers are related to different issues. Some responses indicated concerns that specific medical conditions may impair one's ability to perform essential job tasks. These concerns could be partially alleviated by systematically applying a risk assessment framework to identify the specific tasks that may be affected and communicating the strategy for reducing risks to task or mission completion.

Other responses raised basic concerns of fairness and equality of treatment. Although communication is an important step in promoting positive perceptions of fairness, the literature on organizational fairness (e.g., Colquitt and Zipay, 2015) suggests that Air Force ensure that decisionmaking is systematic and transparent, and decision rules are applied equally and consistently to all recruits and airmen. Other critical steps to promote fairness include providing sufficient opportunities for voicing concerns and providing training and education that focus on respect (Colquitt and Zipay, 2015). As concerns are raised, clear explanation and justification must be provided for how and why decisions were made.

Although some concerns may reflect accurate perceptions of others' capabilities, many others might be influenced by biases and misinformation. In addition to combating these misperceptions through training and education, research and our survey results suggest that high-quality interactions with individuals who have medical conditions is related to more-positive attitudes and lower levels of discrimination (e.g., Pettigrew and Tropp, 2006; Turner et al., 2008). Therefore, increasing these positive interactions (e.g., working on teams with shared goals) can lead to higher levels of cultural acceptability.

Evaluate the Potential Benefits and Consequences of a Fully Tailored Medical Standard

Once fairness concerns are addressed, the Air Force may wish to implement tailored medical standards. Prior to implementation, the Air Force should consider one or more trial tests. We suggest incremental trials and offer options, from least to most intensive in terms of resources and risk.

Option 1: Limited Term Waiver for Temporary Condition

A basic trial would tailor one accession standard for a medical or physical condition that can be improved (e.g., overweight). The standard (maximum weight based on height) would be applied to one or more enlisted career fields with guaranteed contracts and facing recruiting difficulties. Selection of the career fields for the trial would require buy-in from the career field managers and other leadership. The Air Force would only temporarily waive the condition. Individuals would be expected to meet the standard once they get through technical training and into their career fields. The tailored standard would be applied by the Air Force accession waiver authority if the waiver authority is given information on the career fields selected for the trial study. The Air Force would then track the outcomes for the individuals who entered on the waived condition versus those who were not, both within the same career field and across career fields. The Air Force would have to track for at least the period during which the waiver applies.

A variant on a basic trial would add a compensatory feature. Instead of allowing the selected individuals to enter solely based on waiving the requirement, they would have to take an additional assessment. For example, the applicants randomly selected for the weight waiver would take a 1.5-mile run test and have to meet specific run-time standards before being waived. The run-time standards could be set at a level that ensures applicants have a realistic chance to gradually improve their fitness over time to meet BMT standards. The Air Force would track outcomes for the trial test "experimental" group compared with other applicants.[14]

In either version, the Air Force could decide if they provide additional supports during training (e.g., additional fitness program during technical training) to help the individuals in the treatment condition or not provide additional support. In the case of providing additional support, the Air Force would want to have another random assignment process so that some individuals get the support and others do not. Adding a support feature to the trial would incur additional cost in terms of the actual support (e.g., cost of building and executing a fitness program) and sample size for the trial.

Option 2: Permanent (or Long-Term) Waiver for Temporary Condition

The Air Force could take Option 1 a step further by permanently waiving the standard or allowing the standard to extend to some designated point (e.g., end of initial term of service). This would mean, in the case of weight, that airmen in the experimental condition would not have to meet the standard weight requirement in any future assessments. The Air Force might also have to provide other waivers that directly tie to the relaxed standard for the experimental group, e.g., waiving certain deployments for airmen who exceed the weight requirement.

Assessment of cultural barriers, such as those examined in our survey, would be particularly important in this type of trial test because different standards would be used within the same career field. Moreover, retention review board processes would have to be modified for the treatment group.

Option 3: Permanent (or Long-Term) Waiver for Permanent Condition

For conditions that are not malleable, such as vision loss from a medical disorder, the Air Force could not provide a temporary waiver (e.g., for individuals not expected to regain vision). Waivers for permanent conditions are somewhat akin to the model used to accommodate persons with disabilities. The Air Force would have to carefully think through work redesign elements, as well as waivers for deployment and other requirements.

---

[14] A similar trial program was implemented by the Army in the mid-2000s; results of the program are discussed by Bedno et al. (2010).

General Conclusion

This report identifies different types of cultural barriers that the Air Force may need to address to successfully tailor medical standards for individuals or career fields. Specifically, we developed and fielded a survey experiment, and held discussions with key stakeholders to identify both anticipated benefits of tailored standards and potential barriers to implementation. Although our findings suggest cultural barriers may exist, we offer options for the Air Force to pave a path ahead if they wish to tailor medical standards, particularly as biomarker technologies improve and present opportunities for practical application.

Appendix A. Medical Standards for Air Force Cyber, Maintenance, and Remotely Piloted Aircraft

This appendix provides examples of medical standards for various cyber, aircraft maintenance, and RPA career fields in the Air Force. This information is designed to provide readers with a general understanding of the variation in medical standards across Air Force career fields.

Table A.1 provides a high-level summary of accession and retention medical standards by career field and AFSC. Additional discussion follows the table.

Table A.1. Summary of Medical Standards for Select Cyber, Aircraft Maintenance, and Remotely Piloted Aircraft Career Fields

Career Field	AFSC	Summary of Key Points
Cyber	Officer: 17X Enlisted: 3D0XX, 1B4X1, 3D1XX	• Generally, minimal additional medical standards are required beyond general Air Force–wide entry requirements • A few AFSCs have more-stringent physical strength and psychiatric stability requirements

Tactical Aircraft Maintenance	Enlisted: 2A3X1	• Compared with general Air Force–wide entry requirements, this specialty has more-stringent entry requirements:
		  o Strength Aptitude Test (SAT) (70 pounds)[a]
		  o Normal hearing and psychiatric stability (PULHES "H" = 1, "S" = 1 or 2)[b]
		  o Normal color vision

RPA	Officer: 18EX, 18GX, 18SX Enlisted: 1U0X1, 1U1X1	• For enlisted AFSCs, applicants can have little or no issues with their physical condition (P), upper extremities (U), lower extremities (L), hearing (H), vision (eyes) (E), and psychiatric stability (S). • Additional medical standards are required for enlisted and officer AFSCs associated with aircraft operations.

NOTES: AFSCs with an "X" are placeholders for multiple skill levels or specialties.
[a] The SAT is a "weight-lifting test performed on an incremental lifting machine similar to equipment found in fitness centers. The test requires recruits to lift increasingly heavier weights until they either fail to lift the weight or they meet the weight requirement for their specific specialty" (Robson et al., 2018, p. viii). The SAT is scored in increments of 10 pounds, with the minimum for entry set at 40 pounds.
[b] PULHES is the acronym used for the Physical Profile Serial Chart. Each letter of PULHES presents a different aspect of the physical profile, as listed in the table (AFI 48-123, 2018). Each letter has an associated score ranging from 1 (reflecting normal condition) to 4 (reflecting significant defects with person likely in a medical review board status).

For **cyber specialties**, medical standards at accession and for retention match the general medical requirements for other specialties. However, there are exceptions. Two enlisted specialties, Cyber Warfare Operations (1B4X1) and Cable and Antenna Systems (3D1X7), require high levels of psychiatric stability to maintain security clearances and, therefore, require a psychiatric stability (S in PULHES) equal to 1, which is defined as "Diagnosis or treatment results in no impairment or potential impairment of duty function, risk to the mission or ability to maintain security clearance" (see Table A3.1 in AFI 48-123, 2018).

In addition to psychiatric stability requirements, two enlisted cyber specialties have above-minimum physical standards. Cable and Antenna Systems (3D1X7) requires applicants demonstrate the ability to lift 80 pounds on the SAT. This specialty also requires that applicants have normal lower extremities (PULHES L = 1). RF (Radio Frequency) Transmission Systems (3D1X3) also requires applicants achieve a higher-than-minimum SAT score of 70 pounds.

The enlisted specialty of **Tactical Aircraft Maintenance** (2A3X1) mostly follows general Air Force medical requirements with some exceptions for physical strength, hearing, vision, and psychiatric stability. Specifically, this specialty requires applicants to lift 70 pounds on the SAT and have normal hearing (PULHES H = 1), low risk of psychiatric impairment (PULHES S = 1 or 2), and normal color vision.[15]

Finally, **RPA specialties** have higher medical standards than cyber and maintenance because of requirements related to aircraft operations. RPA pilots must meet the greatest number of medical standards among these career fields, followed by sensor operators, who must meet the medical standards for Ground Based Controllers. For example, RPA pilots must meet air vehicle operator duty medical standards, but they do not need the depth perception or ability to withstand ear pressurization required of manned pilots. RPA pilots also need to attain flying class II status at Pueblo (manned aircraft training as part of undergraduate RPA training) but can get waivers after that. In contrast, RPA sensor operators need normal color vision and must pass the Ground Based Aircraft Controller Physical.

Applicants for the two enlisted RPA specialties (Sensor Operator 1U0X1, Pilot 1U1X1) also require normal levels or low levels of issues for PULHES (i.e., all scores of 1 or 2).

To provide a sense of types of the RPA retention medical standards compared with baseline medical retention standards in the Air Force, we provide Figure A.1. The figure shows the counts of disqualifying conditions by medical category for general Air Force retention and by the two RPA career field categories of pilot and sensor operator. We also provide a summation of the disqualifications in a "Total" category. The counts in the figure are not meant to signify importance of the medical categories but provide a general sense of differences between RPA and baseline medical standards for retention in the Air Force. For example, there are a total of 81 possible disqualifying "Eyes and Vision" conditions. Of those 81, there are 59 conditions considered for retention of RPA pilots and 32 for sensor operators. Because of the vision

---

[15] We also reviewed Maintenance Officer (21AX) medical requirements but did not find any that went above the general requirements.

requirements in these career fields, the "Eyes and Vision" retention standards are higher than general Air Force retention standards.

Figure A.1. Categories of Disqualifying Medical Conditions by Remotely Piloted Aircraft Career Fields and Baseline Air Force Retention

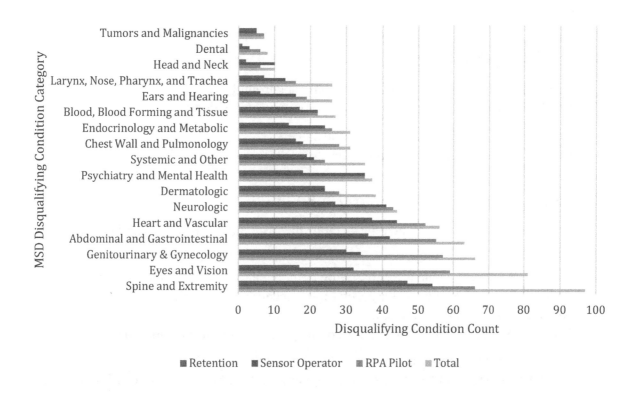

SOURCE: Author calculations based on conditions listed by medical category in the MSD (U.S. Air Force, 2018).

Appendix B. Subject-Matter Expert Question Guide

This appendix provides the questions and follow-up probes used to guide discussions with the SME.

Participant Background

1. Can you briefly describe your professional background?
2. What are the primary responsibilities of your current position?

- How long have you been in this position?
- Have you had similar types of positions before?

Benefits and Limitations of Tailored Standards

3. What value, if any, would there be to tailor medical and/or physical standards in the Air Force?

- *Prompt*: Would the value differ based on component, i.e., Active, Guard, and Reserve?
- *Prompt*: Would the value differ based on the specific career field (e.g., cyber vs. personnel vs. aircraft maintenance)?
- *Prompt:* Would the value differ based on the specific condition/standard?

    a. Missing extremities (arm, leg, hand and/or foot)
    b. Physical health, such as Asthma, Irregular heartbeat (arrhythmia), or Migraines, or being Overweight
    c. Hearing or Vision impairment
    d. Learning or attention challenges (e.g., attention deficit hyperactivity disorder (ADHD or Dyslexia)
    e. Alcohol or Prescription drug addiction
    f. Mental health, such as Depression or posttraumatic stress disorder (PTSD)

- *Prompt*: What value, if any, would there be if individuals unable to meet medical/physical standards served in uniform instead of serving as an Air Force civilian?

4. What would be the major barriers to implementing tailored medical and/or physical standards in the Air Force?

- *Prompt:* How would opinions of Airmen (and other Service's military personnel) change If standards were changed only for certain specialties in the Air Force?
- *Prompt:* What kinds of accommodations, if any, would the Air Force need provide to airmen who do not meet medical/physical standards at accession, assuming those airmen were allowed to serve? Would these accommodations be feasible?
- *Prompt:* Would you expect airmen or leaders to believe those accommodations to be fair? Why or why not?

- *Prompt:* What policies and practices would need to change to successfully implement tailored standards? (e.g., training, deployability requirements, MEPS)?
- *Prompt:* What would the Air Force need to do to overcome any resistance to implementing tailored standards?

Genetic Testing Perceptions

Our last set of questions deviate somewhat from the general question of tailoring medical and physical standards to career field needs. We'd now like to ask about opportunities and challenges the Air Force might face in using genetic testing to support decisions for screening Air Force applicants for military entry.

[Ask participant if he/she is familiar with genetic testing. If not, use the following description: *Genetic testing provides information on a person's DNA. Genetic tests have been used to measure genetic conditions and disorders, but also mental capabilities, such as memory, attention, and spatial ability. Genetic tests are typically conducted using blood samples.*]

Based on your understanding of genetic testing:

5. How do you think genetic testing could be used in the Air Force?
    a. For different objectives?
        i. To provide Air Force applicants with career guidance.
        ii. To inform Air Force applicants of possible genetic disorders.
        iii. To screen out Air Force applicants at risk for physical conditions.
        iv. To screen out Air Force applicants at risk for behavioral disorders.
        v. To assign people entering the Air Force into certain Air Force specialties
        vi. To prevent people joining the Air Force from entering certain Air Force specialties.
        vii. To determine how often Airmen should receive physical fitness assessments.
        viii. Useful for all specialties?

6. What barriers do you think exist in implementing genetic testing for screening recruits into jobs in the Air Force?

    a. Privacy concerns?
    b. Security of information?
    c. Cost to implement?
    d. Resistance from recruiters and/or recruits?

Closing Questions/Comments

Thank you for your time today. Do you have anything else you would like to share about tailoring medical and physical standards to Air Force career field needs?

Appendix C. Hearing Condition Survey: Respondents Provided with Questions About an Airman with Below Standard Hearing

INFORMED CONSENT

Invitation to Participate in RAND Survey on
Recruiting, Training, and Retaining Mission-Capable Airmen

We are asking for your help in better understanding attitudes toward Air Force accession standards, policies, and processes, including maintaining or adding flexibility to enlisted and officer candidate selection and classification (i.e., Air Force Specialty Code [AFSC]). One of the best ways to learn about these topics is by asking Airmen to share their thoughts. You are one of a small number of Airmen selected to help with this research by completing a survey.

The Air Force's Office of the Surgeon General (AF/SG) commissioned the RAND Corporation to conduct a survey. The survey contains questions addressing alternative career paths, tailored accession standards, and new technologies for Air Force selection and classification. All responses will be anonymous, such that we will not be able to connect your survey responses to you. We expect the survey to take about 20 minutes to complete.

WHAT IS RAND? The RAND Corporation is a non-profit research institution that conducts research for the Office of the Secretary of Defense (OSD), the Services, and other Department of Defense research sponsors. Information about RAND is available at www.rand.org.

WHY IS RAND DOING A SURVEY? RAND is conducting research examining either maintaining or changing current accession standards, policies, and processes to meet manning requirements and performance optimization. This is an approved survey:
https://www.my.af.mil/gcss-af/USAF/ep/globalTab.do?channelPageId=sE3494DD04562FCC901456BE0545C017A

HOW WAS I CHOSEN? You were asked to complete this survey because you are in a career field, or completing training related to a career field, that is under preliminary consideration for potential modification to accession standards, policies, or processes.

WHAT DOES PARTICIPATION ENTAIL? The paper-based survey is expected to take 20 minutes to complete.

DO I HAVE TO PARTICIPATE? The survey is completely voluntary. There is no penalty if you decide not to complete the survey or choose not to respond to certain questions within the survey. RAND has asked you to participate because the study findings will inform crucial decisions regarding Air Force accession policies. In addition, Air Force leaders are very interested in understanding your views on this topic. If you choose to participate, do NOT discuss or comment on classified or operationally sensitive information.

WHAT WILL BE DONE WITH MY SURVEY RESPONSES? This is an anonymous survey, so please do not write identifying information, such as your name, on the survey. Your responses will not be connected to you, and your responses will be combined with information from other respondents. Comments from open-ended (write-in) questions may be reported word for word, but never with identifiable information. No Air Force military personnel will see your individual survey responses, nor will RAND release any data that could identify you to anyone in the Air Force, any DoD agencies, or anyone else, except as required by law. However, please note that we cannot provide confidentiality to a participant regarding comments involving criminal activity/behavior, or statements that pose a threat to yourself or others.

IF YOU HAVE READ THE INFORMATION ABOVE AND CONSENT TO PARTICIPATE IN THIS STUDY, PLEASE CONTINUE TO THE NEXT PAGE. IF YOU PREFER NOT TO PARTICIPATE, PLEASE TURN YOUR BLANK SURVEY IN NOW.

For more information about this project, please contact either one of the project leaders:

Dr. Sean Robson	Dr. Maria Lytell
1200 South Hayes Street	1200 South Hayes Street
Arlington, VA 22202-5050	Arlington, VA 22202-5050
Telephone: 703-413-1100 x5228	Telephone: 703-413-1100 x5238
Email: smrobson@rand.org	Email: mlytell@rand.org

You may also contact the study's official Air Force action officer:
Col. Martin LaFrance (HAF/SG/3/5A)
Telephone: 703-681-6680
DSN: 761-6880
Email: martin.w.lafrance@mail.mil

In this section, please imagine that an Airman Basic (E1) in your career field, named Thompson, has been assigned to your unit. When he joined the Air Force, Thompson's hearing was below the current Air Force hearing standards – partial hearing. He met all other current requirements to join the Air Force. Thompson's hearing has stayed about the same since he joined. He meets all other current Air Force standards. Thompson is able to perform all essential job duties. However, Thompson is not eligible to deploy to some locations because he does not meet the hearing standards for those deployed locations.

Please indicate your level of agreement or disagreement with the statements about Thompson's hearing below.

Thompson's hearing ...	Disagree Strongly	Disagree	Neither Agree nor Disagree	Agree	Agree Strongly
A1. ... will put coworkers at risk.	1 ☐	2 ☐	3 ☐	4 ☐	5 ☐
A2. ... will cause problems with coworker relations.	1 ☐	2 ☐	3 ☐	4 ☐	5 ☐
A3. ... will make him difficult to work with.	1 ☐	2 ☐	3 ☐	4 ☐	5 ☐
A4. ... strongly impairs his functioning in life.	1 ☐	2 ☐	3 ☐	4 ☐	5 ☐
A5. ... will make people try to avoid him.	1 ☐	2 ☐	3 ☐	4 ☐	5 ☐
A6. ... makes it difficult to form friendships.	1 ☐	2 ☐	3 ☐	4 ☐	5 ☐
A7. ... will make coworkers uncomfortable.	1 ☐	2 ☐	3 ☐	4 ☐	5 ☐
A8. ... is something he could have prevented.	1 ☐	2 ☐	3 ☐	4 ☐	5 ☐
A9. ... is his own fault.	1 ☐	2 ☐	3 ☐	4 ☐	5 ☐
A10. ...will cause leaders to give him unwanted attention.	1 ☐	2 ☐	3 ☐	4 ☐	5 ☐
A11. ...will cause leaders to ignore him.	1 ☐	2 ☐	3 ☐	4 ☐	5 ☐

As Thompson's coworker, how would you feel about Thompson not deploying when others in your unit deploy? For each pair of adjectives below, please check the number that most closely represents your feeling.

A12.	Fair	1 ☐	2 ☐	3 ☐	4 ☐	5 ☐	Unfair
A13.	Necessary	1 ☐	2 ☐	3 ☐	4 ☐	5 ☐	Unnecessary
A14.	Reasonable	1 ☐	2 ☐	3 ☐	4 ☐	5 ☐	Unreasonable
A15.	Positive	1 ☐	2 ☐	3 ☐	4 ☐	5 ☐	Negative
A16.	Just	1 ☐	2 ☐	3 ☐	4 ☐	5 ☐	Unjust
A17.	Deserved	1 ☐	2 ☐	3 ☐	4 ☐	5 ☐	Undeserved

Please provide your evaluations of Thompson using the scale below.

	Extremely Low	Low	Neither Low nor High	High	Extremely High
A18. Quality of performance on core job tasks	1 ☐	2 ☐	3 ☐	4 ☐	5 ☐
A19. Potential for providing high quality outputs	1 ☐	2 ☐	3 ☐	4 ☐	5 ☐
A20. Potential for providing a high number of outputs	1 ☐	2 ☐	3 ☐	4 ☐	5 ☐
A21. Likelihood of separating	1 ☐	2 ☐	3 ☐	4 ☐	5 ☐
A22. Likelihood of missing work	1 ☐	2 ☐	3 ☐	4 ☐	5 ☐
A23. Potential for being late to work	1 ☐	2 ☐	3 ☐	4 ☐	5 ☐
A24. Potential for getting along with coworkers	1 ☐	2 ☐	3 ☐	4 ☐	5 ☐
A25. Potential for promotion	1 ☐	2 ☐	3 ☐	4 ☐	5 ☐
A26. Work motivation	1 ☐	2 ☐	3 ☐	4 ☐	5 ☐
A27. Health	1 ☐	2 ☐	3 ☐	4 ☐	5 ☐
A28. Ability to handle several tasks at once	1 ☐	2 ☐	3 ☐	4 ☐	5 ☐
A29. Attention to detail	1 ☐	2 ☐	3 ☐	4 ☐	5 ☐
A30. Ability to lead other Airmen	1 ☐	2 ☐	3 ☐	4 ☐	5 ☐
A31. Ability to handle challenging job assignments	1 ☐	2 ☐	3 ☐	4 ☐	5 ☐

	Extremely Low	Low	Neither Low nor High	High	Extremely High
A32. Ability to gain trust of other Airmen	1 ☐	2 ☐	3 ☐	4 ☐	5 ☐
A33. Ability to maintain self-discipline	1 ☐	2 ☐	3 ☐	4 ☐	5 ☐
A34. Ability to put in long work hours	1 ☐	2 ☐	3 ☐	4 ☐	5 ☐
A35. Ability to be handle stress	1 ☐	2 ☐	3 ☐	4 ☐	5 ☐
A36. Likelihood to demonstrate high levels of self-confidence	1 ☐	2 ☐	3 ☐	4 ☐	5 ☐
A37. Ability to set a good example	1 ☐	2 ☐	3 ☐	4 ☐	5 ☐

Please indicate your level of agreement or disagreement with the statements below.

	Disagree Strongly	Disagree	Neither Agree nor Disagree	Agree	Agree Strongly
A38. Thompson should <u>NOT</u> be promoted over other Air Force members of similar performance quality who meet the hearing standards.	1 ☐	2 ☐	3 ☐	4 ☐	5 ☐
A39. Among those who perform equally, Thompson should be the first to go during a reduction in force.	1 ☐	2 ☐	3 ☐	4 ☐	5 ☐
A40. The Air Force should avoid allowing people with Thompson's hearing to join.	1 ☐	2 ☐	3 ☐	4 ☐	5 ☐
A41. The Air Force should hire people with Thompson's hearing as civilians, not as active-duty Airmen.	1 ☐	2 ☐	3 ☐	4 ☐	5 ☐
A42. The Air Force should hire people with Thompson's hearing as Guard or Reserve, not as active-duty Airmen.	1 ☐	2 ☐	3 ☐	4 ☐	5 ☐
A43. The Air Force should avoid hiring people with Thompson's hearing, unless Thompson has higher than average technical skills	1 ☐	2 ☐	3 ☐	4 ☐	5 ☐

A44. People might have different opinions about hearing for different Air Force specialties. If people with Thompson's hearing were only assigned to a set of specialties, how would opinions about this set of specialties change?

Greatly Decrease Opinions	Decrease Opinions	No Effect on Opinions	Improve Opinions	Greatly Improve Opinions
1 ☐	2 ☐	3 ☐	4 ☐	5 ☐

A45. People might also have different opinions about hearing across different military services. If people with Thompson's hearing were only assigned to the Air Force, how would the opinions about the Air Force change among those in other military services?

Greatly Decrease Opinions	Decrease Opinions	No Effect on Opinions	Improve Opinions	Greatly Improve Opinions
1 ☐	2 ☐	3 ☐	4 ☐	5 ☐

Please indicate your level of agreement or disagreement with the statements below. How do you think active-duty enlisted personnel in the Air Force would behave toward Airmen with hearing issues?

Active-duty enlisted personnel in the Air Force would...	Never	Somewhat Infrequently	Neither Infrequently nor Frequently	Somewhat Frequently	All the Time
B1...**ignore** Airmen with hearing issues.	1 ☐	2 ☐	3 ☐	4 ☐	5 ☐
B2...**exclude** Airmen with hearing issues.	1 ☐	2 ☐	3 ☐	4 ☐	5 ☐
B3...**cooperate with** Airmen with hearing issues.	1 ☐	2 ☐	3 ☐	4 ☐	5 ☐
B4...**associate with** Airmen with hearing issues.	1 ☐	2 ☐	3 ☐	4 ☐	5 ☐
B5...**harass** Airmen with hearing issues.	1 ☐	2 ☐	3 ☐	4 ☐	5 ☐
B6...**argue with** Airmen with hearing issues.	1 ☐	2 ☐	3 ☐	4 ☐	5 ☐
B7...**help** Airmen with hearing issues.	1 ☐	2 ☐	3 ☐	4 ☐	5 ☐
B8...**assist** Airmen with hearing issues.	1 ☐	2 ☐	3 ☐	4 ☐	5 ☐

Please indicate the value that best represents how <u>YOU</u> feel toward Airmen with hearing issues.

	Disagree Strongly	Disagree	Neither Agree nor Disagree	Agree	Agree Strongly
B9. I believe that Airmen with hearing issues slow down the rate at which work is completed.	1 ☐	2 ☐	3 ☐	4 ☐	5 ☐
B10. I believe that Airmen with hearing issues require high levels of supervision.	1 ☐	2 ☐	3 ☐	4 ☐	5 ☐
B11. I would feel embarrassed about working with an Airman with hearing issues.	1 ☐	2 ☐	3 ☐	4 ☐	5 ☐
B12. I would feel uncomfortable about working with an Airman with hearing issues.	1 ☐	2 ☐	3 ☐	4 ☐	5 ☐
B13. Providing accommodations to Airmen with hearing issues is not fair to others who do not have those issues.	1 ☐	2 ☐	3 ☐	4 ☐	5 ☐
B14. In the past, Airmen with hearing issues have not received accommodations, and therefore it is not fair to give them accommodations now.	1 ☐	2 ☐	3 ☐	4 ☐	5 ☐

Please indicate whether an Airman with each condition listed below could or could not perform essential job tasks in your unit.

	NO. An Airman with this condition <u>COULD NOT</u> perform essential job tasks.	YES. An Airman with this condition <u>COULD</u> perform essential job tasks.
B15. Missing extremities (arm, leg, hand and/or foot)	1 ☐	2 ☐
B16. Asthma	1 ☐	2 ☐
B17. Overweight	1 ☐	2 ☐
B18. Irregular heartbeat (arrhythmia)	1 ☐	2 ☐
B16. Hearing impairment	1 ☐	2 ☐
B17. Vision impairment	1 ☐	2 ☐
B18. Attention Deficit Hyperactivity Disorder (ADHD)	1 ☐	2 ☐

	NO. *An Airman with this condition <u>COULD NOT</u> perform essential job tasks.*	YES. *An Airman with this condition <u>COULD</u> perform essential job tasks.*
B19. Dyslexia	1 ☐	2 ☐
B20. Alcohol addiction	1 ☐	2 ☐
B21. Prescription drug addiction	1 ☐	2 ☐
B22. Migraines	1 ☐	2 ☐
B23. Depression	1 ☐	2 ☐
B24. Posttraumatic Stress Disorder (PTSD)	1 ☐	2 ☐

Please indicate whether you would or would not feel comfortable working with an Airman with each condition listed below.

	NO. *I <u>WOULD NOT</u> feel comfortable working with an Airman with this condition.*	YES. *I <u>WOULD</u> feel comfortable working with an Airman with this condition.*
B25. Missing extremities (arm, leg, hand and/or foot)	1 ☐	2 ☐
B26. Asthma	1 ☐	2 ☐
B27. Overweight	1 ☐	2 ☐
B28. Irregular heartbeat (arrhythmia)	1 ☐	2 ☐
B29. Hearing impairment	1 ☐	2 ☐
B30. Vision impairment	1 ☐	2 ☐

Please continue to indicate whether you would or would not feel comfortable working with an Airman with each condition listed below.

	NO. I <u>WOULD NOT</u> feel comfortable working with an Airman with this condition.	YES. I <u>WOULD</u> feel comfortable working with an Airman with this condition.
B31. Attention Deficit Hyperactivity Disorder (ADHD)	1 ☐	2 ☐
B32. Dyslexia	1 ☐	2 ☐
B33. Alcohol addiction	1 ☐	2 ☐
B34. Prescription drug addiction	1 ☐	2 ☐
B35. Migraines	1 ☐	2 ☐
B36. Depression	1 ☐	2 ☐
B37. Posttraumatic Stress Disorder (PTSD)	1 ☐	2 ☐

The next set of questions address your experiences with individuals who have hearing issues. Please respond using the provided scales and response options.

C1. During your entire work history, including time inside and outside the Air Force, how <u>frequently</u> have you worked with coworkers who have had hearing issues?

Never	Rarely	Sometimes	Often	Quite A Lot	Not Applicable/ Don't Know
1 ☐	2 ☐	3 ☐	4 ☐	5 ☐	8 ☐

C2. During your entire work history, including time inside and outside the Air Force, what has the <u>quality of your interactions</u> with your coworkers who have had hearing issues been like?

Very Poor	Poor	Fair	Good	Excellent	Not Applicable/Don't Know
1 ☐	2 ☐	3 ☐	4 ☐	5 ☐	8 ☐

C3. Do you currently work with at least one civilian or contractor who has hearing issues?

₁ ☐ Yes

₂ ☐ No

₈ ☐ Not Sure/Not Applicable

C4. Do you currently work with at least one uniformed military person who has hearing issues?

1 ☐ Yes

2 ☐ No

8 ☐ Not Sure/Not Applicable

C5. Do you know any other person (not a coworker) who has hearing issues?

1 ☐ Yes

2 ☐ No

8 ☐ Not Sure/Not Applicable

Some organizations may consider genetic testing to assess a job applicant's potential to perform well in a job. Genetic testing provides information on a person's DNA. Genetic tests have been used to measure genetic conditions and disorders, but also mental capabilities, such as memory, attention, and spatial ability. Genetic tests are typically conducted using blood samples.

Based on your understanding of genetic tests, please indicate the value that best represents how you would feel about the Air Force using genetic tests to support decisions for screening Air Force applicants for <u>military entry</u>.

	Disagree Strongly	Disagree	Neither Agree nor Disagree	Agree	Agree Strongly
D1. Genetic testing would accurately indicate whether an Air Force applicant would perform well in a cognitively demanding specialty.	1 ☐	2 ☐	3 ☐	4 ☐	5 ☐
D2. Genetic testing would accurately indicate whether an Air Force applicant has mental capabilities to serve in the Air Force.	1 ☐	2 ☐	3 ☐	4 ☐	5 ☐
D3. Genetic testing is an invasion of an Air Force applicant's privacy.	1 ☐	2 ☐	3 ☐	4 ☐	5 ☐
D4. The results of a genetic test would reveal personal medical information that the Air Force has no right to know.	1 ☐	2 ☐	3 ☐	4 ☐	5 ☐
D5. Genetic testing would be an effective means of screening Air Force applicants.	1 ☐	2 ☐	3 ☐	4 ☐	5 ☐

	Disagree Strongly	Disagree	Neither Agree nor Disagree	Agree	Agree Strongly
D6. The expenses incurred by administering and interpreting genetic tests are a sound investment for the Air Force.	1 ☐	2 ☐	3 ☐	4 ☐	5 ☐
D7. Genetic testing would be a sensible way to screen Air Force applicants.	1 ☐	2 ☐	3 ☐	4 ☐	5 ☐
D8. Genetic testing would show that the Air Force treats its applicants fairly.	1 ☐	2 ☐	3 ☐	4 ☐	5 ☐
D9. I believe that genetic testing implemented by the Air Force for screening applicants would be fair.	1 ☐	2 ☐	3 ☐	4 ☐	5 ☐
D10. If I were offered the chance to submit an anonymous letter protesting using genetic tests to screen Air Force applicants, I would do so.	1 ☐	2 ☐	3 ☐	4 ☐	5 ☐
D11. If I had the chance, I would file a formal protest regarding the Air Force using genetic tests to screen applicants.	1 ☐	2 ☐	3 ☐	4 ☐	5 ☐

Organizations could use genetic testing results for many purposes. Would you oppose or support the Air Force using the results of genetic tests for each purpose listed below?

How would you feel about the Air Force using individuals' genetic test results to…	OPPOSE. I would oppose the Air Force using genetic testing results for this purpose.	SUPPORT. I would support the Air Force using genetic testing results for this purpose.
D12. …provide Air Force applicants with career guidance	1 ☐	2 ☐
D13. …inform Air Force applicants of possible genetic disorders	1 ☐	2 ☐
D14. …screen out Air Force applicants at risk for physical conditions	1 ☐	2 ☐
D15. …screen out Air Force applicants at risk for behavioral disorders	1 ☐	2 ☐
D16. …assign people entering the Air Force into certain Air Force specialties	1 ☐	2 ☐

How would you feel about the Air Force using individuals' genetic test results to...	OPPOSE. I would _oppose_ the Air Force using genetic testing results for this purpose.	SUPPORT. I would _support_ the Air Force using genetic testing results for this purpose.
D17. ...prevent people entering the Air Force from joining certain Air Force specialties	1 ☐	2 ☐
D18. ...determine how often Airmen should receive physical fitness assessments	1 ☐	2 ☐

D19. People have different levels of familiarity with genetic testing. Please use the scale below to indicate your level of familiarity with genetic testing.

Not at all Familiar	_A Little Familiar_	_Somewhat Familiar_	_Quite a Bit Familiar_	_Extremely Familiar_
1 ☐	2 ☐	3 ☐	4 ☐	5 ☐

The questions below address your background. Please respond using the spaces or scales provided.

E1. How old are you? _____

E2. What is your race?

₁ ☐ White

₂ ☐ Black or African American

₃ ☐ American Indian or Alaska Native

₄ ☐ Asian Indian

₅ ☐ Chinese

₆ ☐ Filipino

₇ ☐ Other Asian (for example, Hmong, Laotian, Thai, Pakistani, Cambodian, and so on)

₈ ☐ Native Hawaiian

₉ ☐ Guamanian or Chamorro

₁₀ ☐ Samoan

₁₁ ☐ Other Pacific Islander (for example, Fijian, Tongan, and so on)

E3. Are you of Hispanic, Latino, or Spanish origin?

1 ☐ No, not of Hispanic, Latino, or Spanish origin

2 ☐ Yes, Cuban

3 ☐ Yes, Mexican, Mexican American, Chicano

4 ☐ Yes, Puerto Rican

5 ☐ Yes, another Hispanic, Latino, or Spanish origin

E4. In general, would you say your physical health is:

Very Poor	Poor	Neither Poor nor Good	Good	Very Good
1 ☐	2 ☐	3 ☐	4 ☐	5 ☐

E5. Do you feel you have a hearing issue?

1 ☐ Yes

2 ☐ No

8 ☐ Don't Know

E6. Do you consider yourself to be:

Very Underweight	Underweight	About Right	Overweight	Very Overweight
1 ☐	2 ☐	3 ☐	4 ☐	5 ☐

E7. What is your gender?

1 ☐ Male

2 ☐ Female

3 ☐ Other/Prefer Not to Say

E8. What is the highest degree or level of education that you have completed?

1 ☐ Less than high school

2 ☐ High school diploma/GED

3 ☐ Some college credit, but LESS than 1 year of college credit

4 ☐ 1 or more years of college credit, no degree

5 ☐ Associate's degree (for example, AA, AS)

6 ☐ Bachelor's degree (for example, BA, BS)

7 ☐ Master's degree (for example, MA, MS, MEng, MEd, MSW, MBA)

8 ☐ Professional degree beyond a bachelor's degree (for example, MD, DDS, DVM, LLB, JD)

9 ☐ Doctorate degree (for example, PhD, EdD)

E9. In what year did you first enter active-duty U.S. military service? _____

Entry Year

E10. What is your current pay grade?

1 ☐ E1	10 ☐ O-1/O-1E
2 ☐ E2	11 ☐ O-2/O-2E
3 ☐ E3	12 ☐ O-3/O-3E
4 ☐ E4	13 ☐ O4
5 ☐ E5	14 ☐ O5
6 ☐ E6	15 ☐ O6 or above
7 ☐ E7	
8 ☐ E8	
9 ☐ E9	

E11. What is your primary Air Force Specialty Code (AFSC)?

1 ☐ 17XX (Cyber Officer)	8 ☐ 3D1X2 (Cyber Transport Systems)
2 ☐ 1B4X1 (Cyber Warfare Operations)	9 ☐ 3D1X3 (RF Transmission Systems)
3 ☐ 3D0X1 (Knowledge Operations Management)	10 ☐ 3D1X4 (Spectrum Operations)
4 ☐ 3D0X2 (Cyber Systems Operations)	11 ☐ 3D1X7 (Cable and Antenna Systems)
5 ☐ 3D0X3 (Cyber Surety)	12 ☐ Don't Know
6 ☐ 3D0X4 (Computer Systems Programming)	13 ☐ Other_____
7 ☐ 3D1X1 (Client Systems)	Provide or Describe Your AFSC

Appendix D. Additional Information on Survey Methodology and Results

This appendix provides additional details on the survey topic areas and additional results not presented in Chapter 4. For each survey topic area, we present the results for all items broken out by condition (weight versus hearing). We follow with findings of simple comparisons across topic area and also the results of modeling to control for different factors relevant to the survey sample (e.g., tenure in career field). We also provide findings of statistical tests comparing relationships among factors associated with perceptions of genetic testing.

Survey Topic Areas and Item-Level Results

In this section, we describe the survey topic areas, including our sources for survey items and item-level results.

Stigma

Previous research has shown that perceptions of stigma are associated with less coworker acceptance (McLaughlin, Bell, and Stringer, 2004). Coworker acceptance is an important aspect of workplace socialization and subsequent attitudinal commitment to an organization (Dodd-McCue and Wright, 1996; Saks and Ashforth, 1997). We used 11 survey items to operationalize stigma. Eight of these drew from a previously developed measure of stigma (McLaughlin, Bell, and Stringer, 2004), and we created two new items to assess leader responses to this issue. For the 11 items (Figure D.1), participants indicated their level of disagreement or agreement with statements about fictional airman Thompson (1 = Disagree Strongly; 5 = Agree Strongly). These items addressed stigma associated with the performance impact (e.g., "will put coworkers at risk"), social impact (e.g., "will make people try to avoid him"), onset control (e.g., "is something he could have prevented"), and leadership response ("will cause leaders to give him unwanted attention"; "will cause leaders to ignore him") regarding Thompson's issue. Coefficient alpha for this scale was acceptable at $\alpha = .87$.

Figure D.1. Item-Level Survey Results for Stigma, by Hearing and Weight Survey Condition

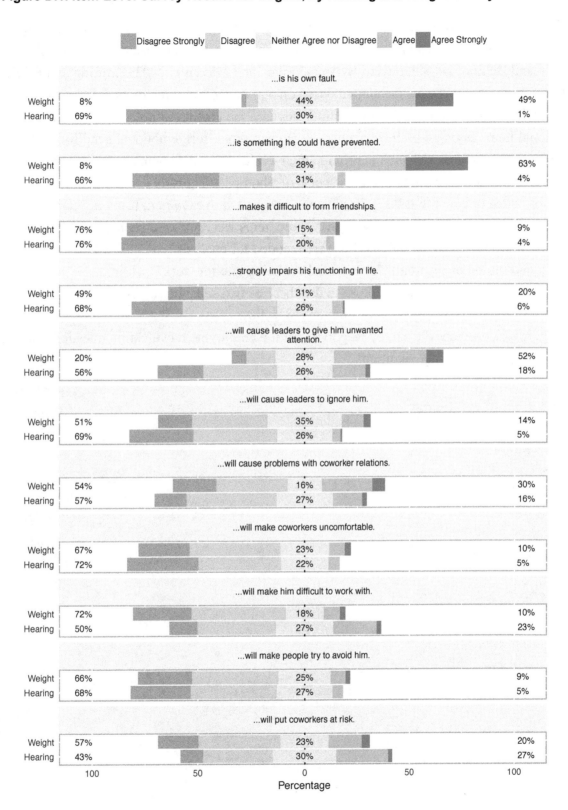

51

Employability Evaluation

We next examined participants' evaluative judgments of Thompson. Ten of these items drew from previously developed measures to examine evaluations of Thompson's employability (Dalgin and Bellino, 2008; Gouvier, Sytsma-Jordan, and Mayville, 2003; Krefting and Brief, 1976). Ten of the items were developed based on a review of research on weight bias (Giel et al., 2010) and included to ensure that evaluations covered the breadth of potential evaluations. Additional items assessed such concepts as demonstrating effort, emotional stability, and self-discipline. We asked participants to provide their evaluations of Thompson and presented them with the 20 items, addressing different aspects of Thompson's job-related abilities (e.g., "quality of performance of core job tasks"). Participants responded to each item using a 5-point scale (1 = Extremely Low; 5 = Extremely High). Three items were reversed such that higher scores were for more negative evaluations and were recoded for analysis (e.g., "likelihood of missing work"; "likelihood of separating"; "potential for being late for work"). Ultimately, given the different origins of the items, we chose to use these as two separate scales, employability evaluations (α = .87), and general evaluations (α = .96).

Figure D.2 provides the survey responses for the employment evaluation questions, separated by the weight and hearing conditions.

Figure D.2. Item-Level Survey Results for Employability Evaluation, by Hearing and Weight Survey Condition

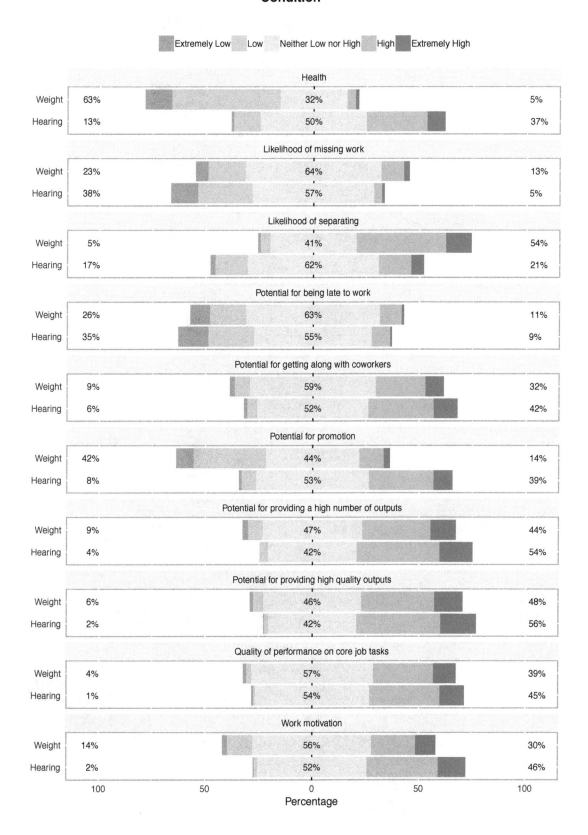

Figure D.2–Continued

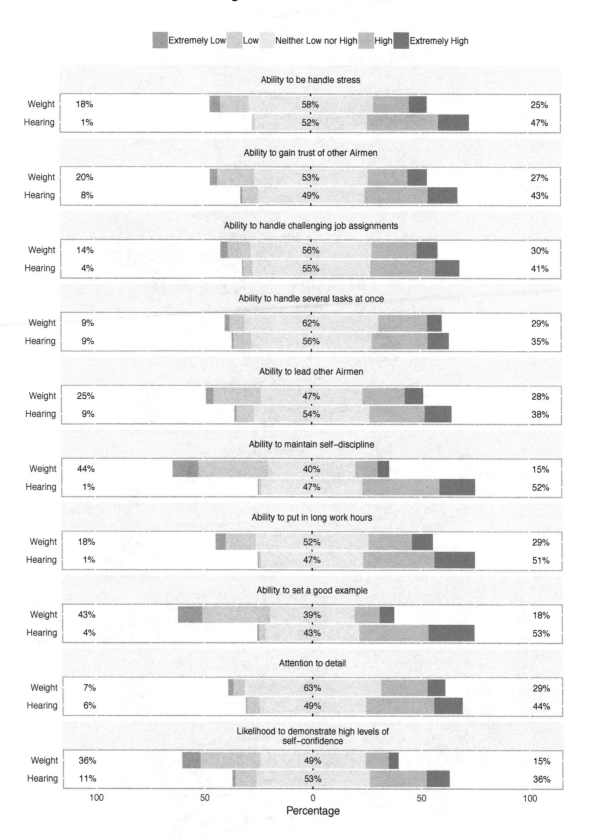

Discriminatory Judgments and Perceived Impact on Career Fields and Service

The next set of items addressed participants' discriminatory employment judgments regarding Thompson. Three of these items were similar to a previously developed measure of this construct (e.g., "The Air Force should avoid allowing people with Thompson's [weight/hearing] to join") (McLaughlin, Bell, and Stringer, 2004). We also developed three additional times to address employment perceptions specific to the Air Force (e.g., "The Air Force should hire people with Thompson's [weight/hearing] as civilians, not as active-duty airmen," "The Air Force should hire people with Thompson's [weight/hearing] as Guard or Reserve, not as active-duty airmen," "The Air Force should avoid hiring people with Thompson's [weight/hearing], unless Thompson has higher than average technical skills"). Participants responded to all six items using a 5-point scale (1 = Disagree Strongly; 5 = Agree Strongly). Coefficient alpha for these six items was acceptable at $\alpha = .78$.

We asked two questions to address the perceived impact of assigning people with Thompson's issue to certain specialties and assigning people with Thompson's issue to one service would have on opinions of those specialties or that service, respectively. Specifically, we asked, "If people with Thompson's [weight/hearing] were only assigned to a set of specialties, how would opinions about this set of specialties change?" We also asked, "If people with Thompson's [weight/hearing] were only assigned to the Air Force, how would the opinions about the Air Force change among those in other military services?" Participants responded to each question using a 5-point scale (1 = Greatly Decrease Opinions; 5 = Greatly Improve Opinions). These two items were not used as a scale but were examined independently.

Figure D.3 provides the survey responses for the items involving discriminatory judgments and perceived impact on career field or service, separated by the weight and hearing conditions.

Figure D.3. Item-Level Survey Results for Discriminatory Judgements and Perceived Impact on Career Field/Service, by Hearing and Weight Survey Condition

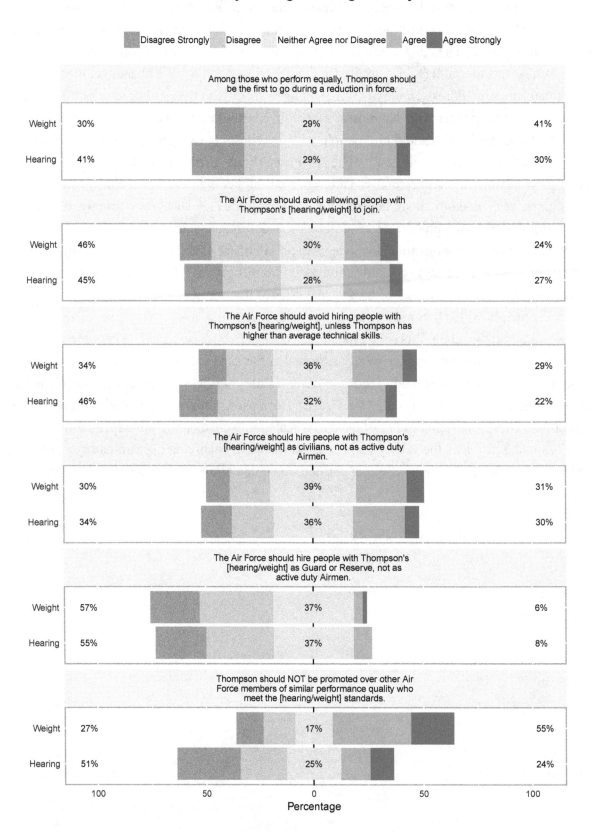

Behavioral Inclinations and Perceptions

The next survey section addressed behavioral inclinations and perceptions toward airmen with various issues.

Active and Passive Facilitation and Harm

We assessed two dimensions of behavioral inclinations, specifically active-passive and facilitation-harm, that participants expected active-duty Air Force officers or enlisted personnel (matched with participant status) to have toward airmen with either weight or hearing issues, depending on survey condition. These dimensions are based on previous research results that suggest there are two dimensions to discriminatory behaviors (Cuddy, Fiske, and Glick, 2007; Cuddy, Fiske, and Glick, 2008). Active behaviors are overt and directed actions, whereas passive behaviors are less targeted. In addition, facilitation encompasses behaviors that assist others, whereas harmful behaviors can be detrimental.

We assessed active facilitation by asking participants to indicate how often active-duty Air Force officers or enlisted personnel (depending on participant status) would assist and help airmen with weight or hearing issues (1 = Never; 5 = All the Time). We assessed active harm by asking participants to indicate how often active-duty Air Force officers or enlisted personnel would harass and argue with airmen with the focus issues (1 = Never; 5 = All the Time). To assess passive facilitation, we asked participants to indicate how often active-duty Air Force officers or enlisted personnel would cooperate with and associate with airmen with weight or hearing issues (1 = Never; 5 = All the Time. To assess passive harm, we asked them to indicate how often active-duty Air Force officers or enlisted personnel would ignore and exclude these individuals (1 = Never; 5 = All the Time). Because there were only two items per dimension, we created subscales for Harm (α = .84) and Facilitation (α = .86), aggregating both active and passive behaviors in each case.

Figures B.4 and B.5 provide the survey responses for the items involving active and passive facilitation (Figure D.4) and harm (Figure D.5), separated by the weight and hearing conditions.

Figure D.4. Item-Level Survey Results for Active and Passive Facilitation, by Hearing and Weight Survey Condition

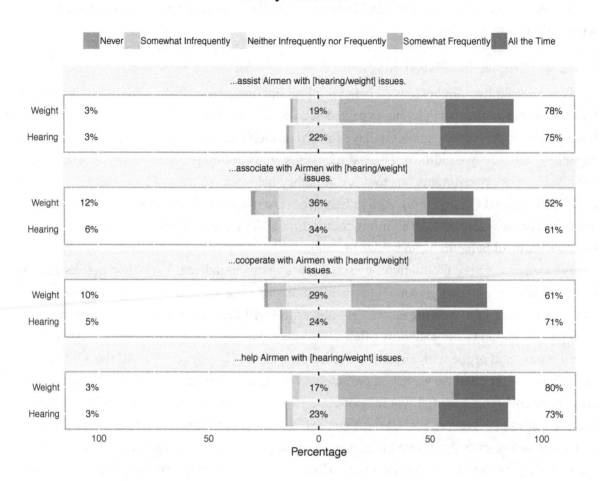

Figure D.5. Item-Level Survey Results for Active and Passive Harm, by Hearing and Weight Survey Condition

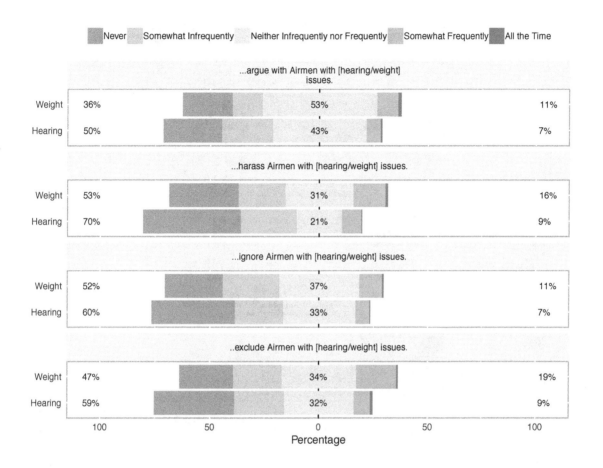

Job-Related Expectancies and Reactions

We next asked participants to respond to six items that addressed their expectations and reactions to airmen with either weight or hearing issues, depending on the survey condition. Two items drew from a previously developed measure of job-related expectancy (e.g., "I believe that Airmen with [weight/hearing] issues slow down the rate at which work is completed"), and two items drew from a previous measure of job-related affective reactions (e.g., "I would feel embarrassed about working with an airman with a [weight/hearing] issue") (Scherbaum, Scherbaum, and Popovich, 2005). The final two items addressed policy fairness, again drawing from a previous measure (e.g., "Providing accommodations to Airmen with [weight/hearing] issues is not fair to employees who do not have those issues") (Grover, 1991). Participants responded to these six items using a 5-point scale (1 = Disagree Strongly; 5 = Agree Strongly). We used these six items as a scale ($\alpha = .85$).

Figure D.6 provides the survey responses for the items involving job-related expectancies and reactions, separated by the weight and hearing conditions.

Figure D.6. Item-Level Survey Results for Job-Related Expectancies and Reactions, by Hearing and Weight Survey Condition

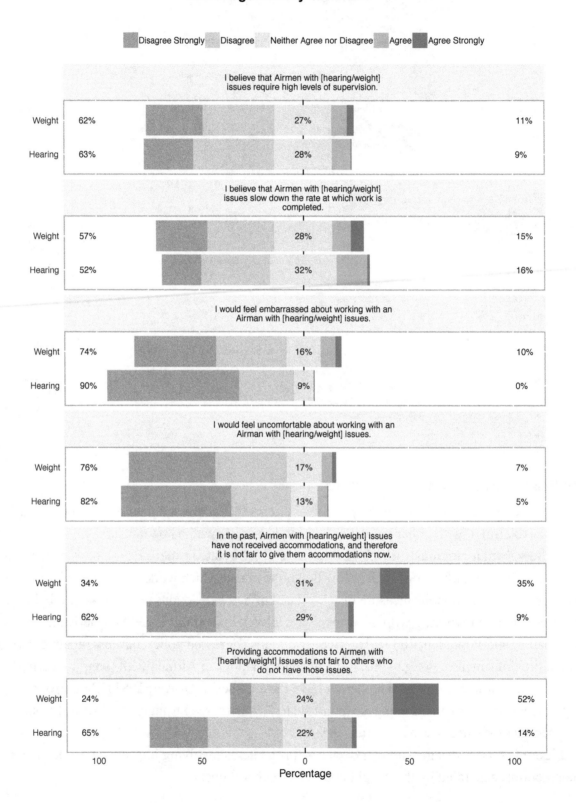

60

Expected Ability and Comfort

We also presented participants with the following 13 conditions: alcohol addiction; asthma; ADHD; depression; dyslexia; hearing impairment; irregular heartbeat (arrhythmia); migraines; missing extremities (arm, leg, hand and/or foot); overweight; PTSD; prescription drug addiction; and vision impairment. We selected conditions based on issues that might disqualify large numbers of individuals from joining the Air Force (Boivin et al., 2016). We asked participants to indicate whether an airman with each condition could perform essential job tasks in his unit. Participants had two response options (1 = No. An airman with this condition could not perform essential job tasks; 2 = Yes. An airman with this condition could perform essential job tasks).

We presented the same 13 conditions a second time and asked participants to indicate whether they would or would not feel comfortable working with an airman with each condition. Participants had two response options (1 = No. I would not feel comfortable working with an Airman with this condition; 2 = Yes. I would feel comfortable working with an airman with this condition).

Figure D.7 provides the survey responses for the items involving expected ability and comfort, separated by the weight and hearing conditions.

Figure D.7. Item-Level Survey Results for Expected Ability and Comfort, by Hearing and Weight Survey Condition

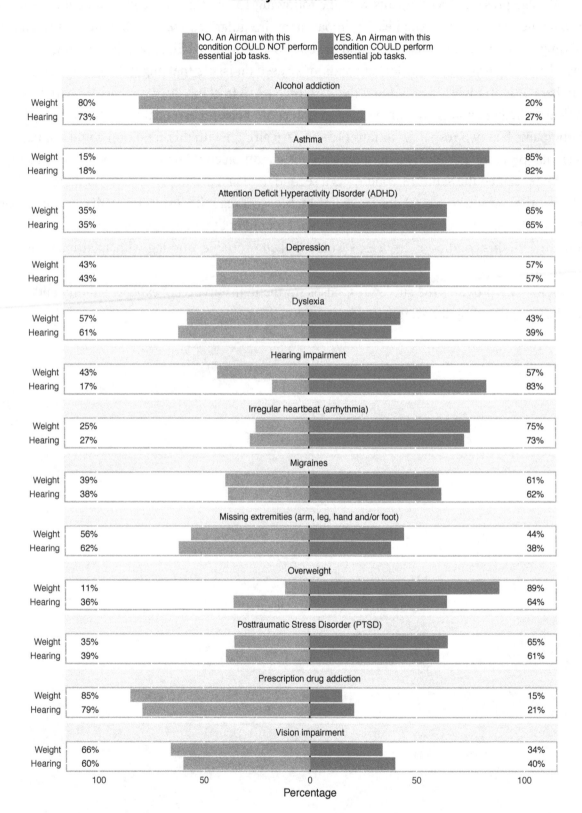

Work Experience

The next set of survey items focused on work history with someone who has had weight or hearing issues, depending on the survey condition. We included these items because previous research suggests that multiple, high-quality interactions with those in another group, such as those with certain conditions, can reduce prejudice and discrimination toward that group (e.g., Pettigrew and Tropp, 2006; Turner et al., 2008). We first asked, "During your entire work history, including time inside and outside the Air Force, how frequently have you worked with coworkers who have had [weight/hearing] issues" (1 = Never; 5 = Quite a Lot; 8 = Not Applicable/Don't Know). Then, we asked "During your entire work history, including time inside and outside the Air Force, what has the quality of your interactions with your coworkers who have had [weight/hearing] issues been like" (1 = Very Poor; 5 = Excellent; 8 = Not Applicable). After that, we asked three additional items addressing whether each participant currently works with at least one civilian or contractor who has weight or hearing issues, whether they currently work with at least one uniformed military person who has weight or hearing issues, and whether they know any other person (not as a coworker) who has weight or hearing issues (1 = Yes; 2 = No; 8 = Not Sure/Not Applicable). Again, these questions either addressed weight or hearing issues, depending on the survey condition to which the participant was randomly assigned.

We combined the items for experience into a 5-point index. First, taking the three items addressing whether participants work with someone or know someone with weight or hearing issues, we summed the number of people with whom participants had current experience (0–3). We then combined that with the item-assessing history to create a scale ranging from 0 (never worked with anyone with [weight/hearing] issues and do not currently work with someone with those issues) to 4 (historically worked often or more and currently know or work with three or more people with [weight/hearing] issues). The midpoint comprised participants who had sometimes worked with someone and currently worked with or knew at least one person.

Figure D.8 provides the survey responses for the items involving experience working with others with weight or hearing issues, separated by the weight and hearing survey conditions. The figure also shows the proportion of responses that were missing or not sure/not applicable versus completed for each item by survey condition. Figure D.9 provides similar information as Figure D.8 but for quality of interactions with coworkers with weight or hearing issues.

Figure D.8. Item-Level Survey Results for Experience Working with Others with Weight or Hearing Issues, by Survey Condition and Proportion Missing Responses

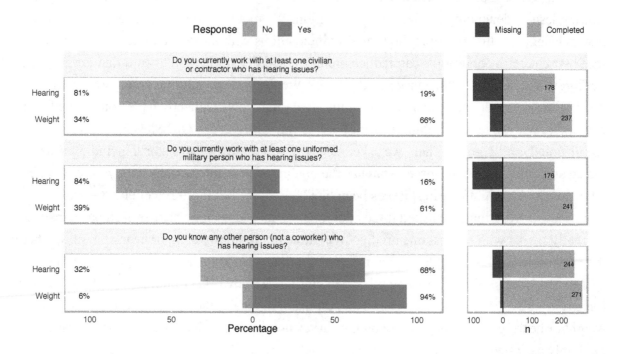

Figure D.9. Item-Level Survey Results for Quality of Experience Working with Others with Weight or Hearing Issues, by Survey Condition and Proportion Missing Responses

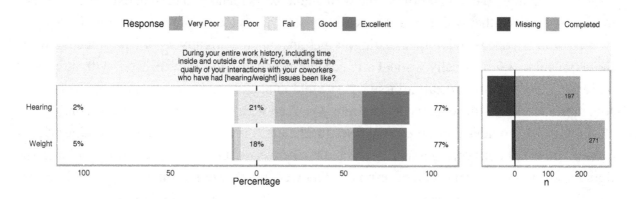

Genetic Testing

One policy option that the Air Force might review involves use of genetic tests to support decisions for screening Air Force applicants for military entry. Therefore, we sought to explore participants' opinions regarding this policy option. We first presented them with 11 items addressing this policy option. The first seven items were based on items previously used to assess attitudes toward fitness for duty testing and drug testing (e.g., "Genetic testing is an invasion of an Air Force applicant's privacy") (Comer, 2000; Comer and Buda, 1996). The next four items addressed perceive fairness of genetic testing (e.g., "Genetic testing would show that

64

the Air Force treats its applicants fairly") and possible responses to genetic testing (e.g., "If I were offered the chance to submit an anonymous letter protesting using genetic tests to screen Air Force applicants, I would do so"), again drawing from measures previously used to assess attitudes toward alcohol and drug testing (Seijts, Skarlicki, and Gilliland, 2003). Participants responded to these 11 items using a 5-point scale (1 = Disagree Strongly; 5 = Agree Strongly). Four items were negatively worded ("Genetic testing is an invasion of an Air Force applicant's privacy"; "The results of a genetic test would reveal personal medical information that the Air Force has no right to know"; "If I were offered the chance to submit an anonymous letter protesting using genetic tests to screen Air Force applicants, I would do so"; and "If I had the chance, I would file a formal protest regarding the Air Force using genetic tests to screen applicants") and were reverse coded for analysis.

There are multiple ways that the Air Force might consider using genetic testing. To address this, we presented participants with seven possible uses of genetic test results and asked how they would feel about the Air Force using individuals' genetic test results for each (e.g., "provide Air Force applicants with career guidance"). Participants indicated whether they opposed or supported each option for using these results (1 = Oppose. I would oppose the Air Force using genetic testing for this purpose; 2 = Support. I would support the Air Force using genetic testing for this purpose). Finally, an individual's level of familiarity might influence their responses to questions regarding genetic testing. Therefore, we also asked participants to indicate their level of familiarity with genetic testing (1 = Not at all Familiar; 5 = Extremely Familiar).

The 11 items on the 5-point scale were examined to determine if they could be used to create an index of attitudes toward genetic testing. We conducted a principal axis factor analysis with varimax rotation. Two factors explained 66 percent of the variance. However, upon examination of the scree plot, it appeared that a one-factor solution was more appropriate. Examination of the factor loadings revealed that the items loading on the second factor were entirely the reverse-coded items, suggesting that rather than being a substantive factor, this second factor was rather an artifact of item phrasing. All item-total correlations were above .53, and coefficient alpha for the items as a whole was high (α = .94), so we combined these 11 items into one index.

For the overall genetics attitudes index, sentiment was not very positive, with an average score of 2.51, which corresponds to mild disagreement with a series of positive statements regarding genetics testing. We also explored whether attitudes toward genetics testing varied by service history characteristics (Table D.1).

Table D.1. Significant Differences on Attitudes Toward Genetics Testing

Factor	Direction	t-test, p < .05
Condition	Personnel in the Hearing condition were more supportive ($\overline{x}$ = 2.59) than were those in the weight condition ($\overline{x}$ = 2.43)	$t(549)$ = 2.02
Commissioning status	Officers and enlisted did not differ	
Cyber-relatedness of career field	Personnel in less cyber-related career fields were more supportive ($\overline{x}$ = 2.65) than those in more cyber-related career fields ($\overline{x}$ = 2.45)	$t(533)$ = 2.35
Approximate tenure	More junior personnel were more supportive ($\overline{x}$ = 2.6) than more senior personnel ($\overline{x}$ = 2.31)	$t(527)$ = 3.44

Moreover, when asked about their support for a variety of potential policy applications of genetic testing, the respondents indicated that the only one that garnered majority support was informing airmen of potential genetic disorders. Clear majorities indicated that they did not support many policy applications of genetic testing, as shown in Table D.2.

Table D.2. Support for Various Policy Applications of Genetic Testing

Purpose of Genetic Test	Percentage Supporting
To prevent people entering the Air Force from joining certain Air Force specialties	25%
To assign people entering the Air Force into certain Air Force specialties	25%
To determine how often Airmen should receive physical fitness assessments	28%
To screen out Air Force applicants at risk for behavioral disorders	38%
To screen out Air Force applicants at risk for physical conditions	44%
To provide Air Force applicants with career guidance	46%
To inform Air Force applicants of possible genetic disorders	80%

Figure D.10 provides the item-level survey responses for attitudes toward genetic testing, separated by the weight and hearing conditions. Figure D.11 provides the same information as Figure D.10 but for questions regarding the Air Force's use of genetic testing.

Figure D.10. Item-Level Survey Results for Attitude Toward Genetic Testing, by Hearing and Weight Survey Condition

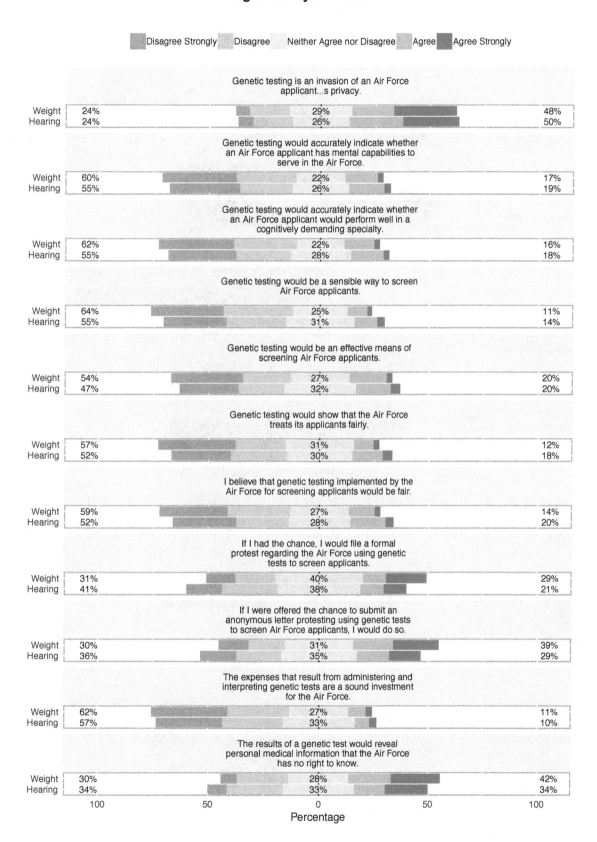

Figure D.11. Item-Level Survey Results for Air Force Use of Genetic Testing, by Hearing and Weight Survey Condition

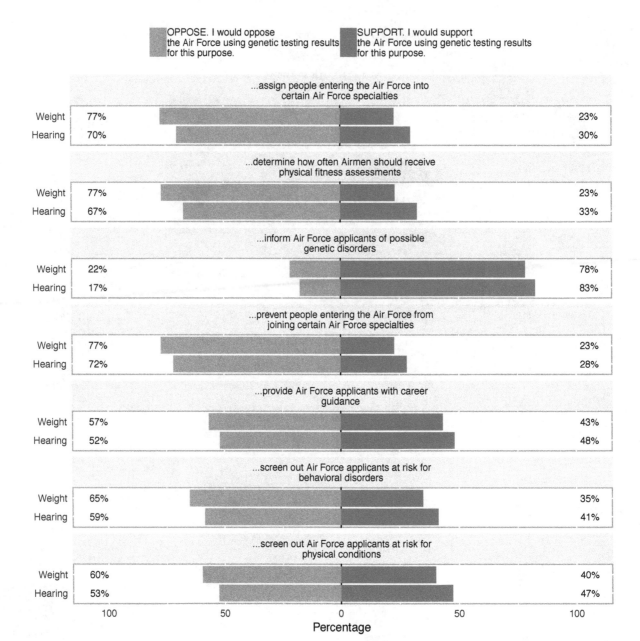

Bibliography

AFI–*See* Air Force Instruction.

Air Force Instruction 36-2905, *Fitness Program*, Washington, D.C.: Department of the Air Force, August 27, 2015. As of September 13, 2018: https://static.e-publishing.af.mil/production/1/af_a1/publication/afman36-2905/afman36-2905.pdf

Air Force Instruction 36-3208, "Subject: Air Force Guidance Memorandum to AFI 36-3208, Administrative Separation of Airmen," Washington, D.C.: Department of the Air Force, June 14, 2018. As of September 19, 2018: http://static.e-publishing.af.mil/production/1/af_a1/publication/afi36-3208/afi36-3208.pdf

Air Force Instruction 36-3212, *Physical Evaluation for Retention, Retirement, and Separation*, Washington, D.C.: Department of the Air Force, November 27, 2009. As of September 19, 2018: http://static.e-publishing.af.mil/production/1/af_a1/publication/afi36-3212/afi36-3212.pdf

Air Force Instruction 48-122, *Deployment Health*, Washington, D.C.: Department of the Air Force, August 18, 2014.

Air Force Instruction 48-123, *Medical Examinations and Standards*, Washington, D.C.: Department of the Air Force, last updated January 28, 2018.

Air Force Personnel Center, *Air Force Enlisted Classification Directory (AFECD): The Official Guide to the Air Force Enlisted Classification Codes*, San Antonio, Texas, October 31, 2017a.

———, *Air Force Officer Classification Directory (AFOCD), The Official Guide to the Air Force Officer Classification Codes*, San Antonio, Texas, October 31, 2017b.

———, "Military Demographics," last updated January 1, 2020. As of October 19, 2020: https://www.afpc.af.mil/Portals/70/documents/03_ABOUT/Military%20Demographics%20Jan%202020.pdf?ver=2020-01-27-093137-550

Baruch, Susannah, and Kathy Hudson, "Civilian and Military Genetics: Nondiscrimination Policy in a Post-GINA World," *American Journal of Human Genetics*, Vol. 83, No. 4, 2008, pp. 435–444.

Bedno, Sheryl A., Christine E. Lang, William E. Daniell, Andrew R. Wiesen, Bennett Datu, and David W. Niebuhr, "Association of Weight at Enlistment with Enrollment in the Army

Weight Control Program and Subsequent Attrition in the Assessment of Recruit Motivation and Strength Study," *Military Medicine*, Vol. 175, No. 3, 2010, pp. 188–193.

Boivin, Michael R., Paul O. Kwan, David N. Cowan, Elizabeth R. Packnett, Xiaoshu Fend, Nadia Garvin, Janice K. Gary, Christine F. Toolin, Michelle M. Yancey, and Yuwie Zhang, *Accession Medical Standards Analysis & Research Activity, (AMSARA), 2016 Annual Report*, Silver Spring, Md.: Walter Reed Army Institute of Research, 2016.

Cawley, John, and Johanna Catherine Maclean, "Unfit for Service: The Implications of Rising Obesity for U.S. Military Recruitment," *Health Economics*, Vol. 21, No. 11, 2012, pp. 1348–1366.

Centers for Disease Control and Prevention, "Defining Adult Overweight and Obesity," webpage, last updated September 17, 2020. As of October 28, 2020: https://www.cdc.gov/obesity/adult/defining.html

Chappelle, Wayne, Kent McDonald, James Christensen, Lillian Prince, Tanya Goodman, William Thompson, and William Hayes, *Sources of Occupational Stress and Prevalence or Burnout and Clinical Distress Among U.S. Air Force Cyber Warfare Operators*, Wright-Patterson Air Force Base, Ohio: Air Force Research Laboratory, 2013.

Chief of Naval Operations Instruction 6110.1J, *Physical Readiness Program*, Washington, D.C.: Department of the Navy, July 11, 2011.

Cohen-Charash, Yochi, and Paul E. Spector, "The Role of Justice in Organizations: A Meta-Analysis," *Organizational Behavior and Human Decision Processes*, Vol. 86, No. 2, 2001, pp. 278–321.

Colquitt, Jason A., Donald E. Conlon, Michael J. Wesson, Christopher O. L. H. Porter, and K. Yee Ng, "Justice at the Millennium: A Meta-Analytic Review of 25 Years of Organizational Justice Research," *Journal of Applied Psychology*, Vol. 86, No. 3, 2001, pp. 425–445.

Colquitt, Jason A., and Kate P. Zipay, "Justice, Fairness, and Employee Reactions," *Annual Review of Organizational Psychology and Organizational Behavior*, Vol. 2, No. 1, 2015, pp. 75–99.

Comer, Debra R., "Employees' Attitudes Toward Fitness-for-Duty Testing," *Journal of Managerial Issues*, Vol. 12, No. 1, 2000, pp. 61–75.

Comer, Debra R., and Richard Buda, "Drug Testers Versus Nontesters: Human Resource Managers' Perceptions and Organizational Characteristics," *Employee Responsibilities and Rights Journal*, Vol. 9, No. 2, 1996, pp. 131–148.

Conti, Gregory, and David Raymond, "Leadership of Cyber Warriors: Enduring Principles and New Directions," *Small Wars Journal*, July 11, 2011.

Cortina, Jose M., "What Is Coefficient Alpha? An Examination of Theory and Applications," *Journal of Applied Psychology*, Vol. 78, No. 1, February 1993, pp. 98–104.

Cuddy, Amy J. C., Susan T. Fiske, and Peter Glick, "The BIAS Map: Behaviors from Intergroup Affect and Stereotypes," *Journal of Personality and Social Psychology*, Vol. 92, No. 4, 2007, pp. 631–648.

———, "Warmth and Competence as Universal Dimensions of Social Perception: The Stereotype Content Model and the BIAS Map," *Advances in Experimental Social Psychology*, Vol. 40, 2008, pp. 61–149.

Dalgin, Rebecca Spirito, and James Bellino, "Invisible Disability Disclosure in an Employment Interview: Impact on Employers' Hiring Decisions and Views of Employability," *Rehabilitation Counseling Bulletin*, Vol. 52, No. 1, 2008, pp. 6–15.

Dall, Timothy M., Yiduo Zhang, Yaozhu J. Chen, Rachel C. Askarinam Wagner, Paul F. Hogan, Nancy K. Fagan, Samuel T. Olaiya, and David N. Tornberg, "Cost Associated with Being Overweight and with Obesity, High Alcohol Consumption, and Tobacco Use Within the Military Health System's TRICARE Prime—Enrolled Population," *American Journal of Health Promotion*, Vol. 22, No. 2, 2007, pp. 120–139.

De Castro, Mauricio, Leslie G. Biesecker, Clesson Turner, Ruth Brenner, Catherine Witkop, Maxwell Mehlman, Chris Bradburne, and Robert C. Green, "Genomic Medicine in the Military," *Genomic Medicine*, Vol. 1, No. 1, 2016, pp. 1–4.

Defense Health Board, "Implications of Trends in Obesity and Overweight for the Department of Defense," Falls Church, Va., November 22, 2013. As of September 19, 2018: http://www.dtic.mil/dtic/tr/fulltext/u2/1027323.pdf

Department of Defense Directive 1308.1, *DoD Physical Fitness and Body Fat Program*, Washington, D.C.: U.S. Department of Defense, June 30, 2004. As of August 30, 2018: http://www.esd.whs.mil/Portals/54/Documents/DD/issuances/dodd/130801p.pdf

Department of Defense Instruction 1308.3, *DoD Physical Fitness and Body Fat Programs Procedures*, Washington, D.C.: U.S. Department of Defense, November 5, 2002. As of September 22, 2018: http://www.esd.whs.mil/Portals/54/Documents/DD/issuances/dodi/130803p.pdf

Department of Defense Instruction 6130.03, *Medical Standards for Appointment, Enlistment, or Induction into the Military Services*, Washington, D.C.: U.S. Department of Defense, May 6, 2018. As of August 30, 2018: http://www.esd.whs.mil/Portals/54/Documents/DD/issuances/dodi/613003p.pdf?ver=2018-05-04-113917-883

Department of Defense Instruction 6490.07, *Deployment-Limiting Medical Conditions for Service Members and DoD Civilian Employees*, Washington, D.C.: U.S. Department of Defense, February 5, 2010. As of September 22, 2018: http://www.esd.whs.mil/Portals/54/Documents/DD/issuances/dodi/649007p.pdf

DoDI—*See* Department of Defense Instruction.

Dodd-McCue, Diane, and Gail B. Wright, "Men, Women, and Attitudinal Commitment: The Effects of Workplace Experiences and Socialization," *Human Relations*, Vol. 49, 1996, pp. 1065–1091.

Fryar, Cheryl D., Margaret D. Carroll, and Cynthia L. Ogden, *Prevalence of Overweight, Obesity, and Extreme Obesity Among Adults: United States, 1960–1962 Through 2011–2012*, Atlanta, Ga.: National Center for Health Statistics, 2014. As of September 22, 2018: https://www.cdc.gov/nchs/data/hestat/obesity_adult_11_12/obesity_adult_11_12.htm

Giel, Katrin Elisabeth, Ansgar Thiel, Martin Teufel, Jochen Mayer, and Stephan Zipfel, "Weight Bias in Work Settings–A Qualitative Review," *Obesity Facts*, Vol. 3, No. 1, 2010, pp. 33–40.

Gilliland, Stephen W., "The Perceived Fairness of Selection Systems: An Organizational Justice Perspective," *Academy of Management Review*, Vol. 18, No. 4, 1993, pp. 694–734.

Gouvier, W. Drew, Sara Sytsma-Jordan, and Stephen Mayville, "Patterns of Discrimination in Hiring Job Applicants With Disabilities: The Role of Disability Type, Job Complexity, and Public Contact," *Rehabilitation Psychology*, Vol. 48, No. 3, 2003, pp. 175–181.

Grover, Steven L., "Predicting the Perceived Fairness of Parental Leave Policies," *Journal of Applied Psychology*, Vol. 76, No. 2, 1991, pp. 247–255.

Henning, Charles, *Army Officer Shortages: Background and Issues for Congress*, Washington, D.C.: Congressional Research Service, 2006. As of September 22, 2018: https://fas.org/sgp/crs/natsec/RL33518.pdf

Jackson, Andrew S., Philip R. Stanforth, Jacques Gagnon, Tuomo Rankinen, Arthur S. Leon, D. C. Rao, James S. Skinner, Claude Bouchard, and Jack H. Wilmore, "The Effect of Sex, Age and Race on Estimating Percentage Body Fat from Body Mass Index: The Heritage Family Study," *International Journal of Obesity*, Vol. 26, No. 6, 2002, pp. 789–796.

Krefting, Linda A., and Arthur P. Brief, "The Impact of Applicant Disability on Evaluative Judgments in the Selection Process," *Academy of Management Journal*, Vol. 19, No. 4, 1976, pp. 675–680.

Krull, Heather, Philip Armour, Kathryn A. Edwards, Kristin Van Abel, Linda Cottrell, and Gulrez Shah Azhar, *The Relationship Between Disability Evaluation and Accession Medical Standards*, Santa Monica, Calif.: RAND Corporation, RR-2429-OSD, 2019. As of December

30, 2019:
https://www.rand.org/pubs/research_reports/RR2429.html

Li, Jennifer J., and Lindsay Daugherty, *Training Cyber Warriors: What Can Be Learned from Defense Language Training?*, Santa Monica, Calif.: RAND Corporation, RR-476-OSD, 2015. As of May 25, 2018:
https://www.rand.org/pubs/research_reports/RR476.html

Marine Corps Order 6110.3A, *Marine Corps Body Composition and Military Appearance Program*, Washington, D.C.: U.S. Department of the Navy, December 15, 2016. As of September 19, 2018:
https://www.marines.mil/Portals/59/Publications/MCO%206110.3A.pdf?ver=2017-01-04-071352-610

McLaughlin, Mary E., Myrtle P. Bell, and Donna Y. Stringer, "Stigma and Acceptance of Persons with Disabilities: Understudied Aspects of Workforce Diversity," *Group and Organization Management*, Vol. 29, No. 3, 2004, pp. 302–333.

National Center for Health Statistics, "National Health and Nutrition Examination Survey," webpage, 2018. As of December 29, 2020:
https://www.cdc.gov/nchs/nhanes/index.htm

Niebuhr, David W., Yuanzhang Li, Timothy E. Powers, Margot R. Krauss, David Chandler, and Thomas Helfer, "Attrition of U.S. Military Enlistees with Waivers for Hearing Deficiency, 1995–2004," *Military Medicine*, Vol. 172, No. 1, 2007, pp. 63–69.

Ogden, Cynthia L., Margaret D. Carroll, Brian K. Kit, and Katherine M. Flegal, "Prevalence of Childhood and Adult Obesity in the United States, 2011–2012," *Journal of American Medical Association*, Vol. 311, No. 8, 2014, pp. 806–814.

Otto, William C., David W. Niebuhr, Timothy E. Powers, Margot R. Krauss, Francis L. McVeigh, and Aaron K. Tarbett, "Attrition of Military Enlistees with a Medical Waiver for Myopia, 1999–2001," *Military Medicine*, Vol. 171, No. 11, November 1, 2006, pp. 1137–1141.

Pettigrew, Thomas F., and Linda R. Tropp, "A Meta-Analytic Test of Intergroup Contact Theory," *Journal of Personality and Social Psychology*, Vol. 90, No. 5, 2006, pp. 751–783.

Reyes-Guzman, Carolyn M., Robert M. Bray, Valerie L. Forman-Hoffman, and Jason Williams, "Overweight and Obesity Trends Among Active Duty Military Personnel: A 13-Year Perspective," *American Journal of Preventive Medicine*, Vol. 48, No. 2, 2015, pp. 145–153.

Robson, Sean, Stephanie Pezard, Maria C. Lytell, Carra S. Sims, John E. Boon, Jr., Jason Michel Etchegaray, Michael Robbins, David Schulker, Jerry M. Sollinger, Jason H. Campbell, Anthony Atler, Stephan B. Seabrook, Deborah L. Gebhardt, Todd A. Baker, Erica K. Volpe, and Kathryn A. Linnenkohl, *Evaluation of the Strength Aptitude Test and Other Fitness Tests to Qualify Air Force Recruits for Physically Demanding Specialties*, Santa Monica, Calif.: RAND Corporation, RR-1789-AF, 2018. As of September 18, 2018: https://www.rand.org/pubs/research_reports/RR1789.html

Rothstein, Mark A., Jessica Roberts, and Tee L. Guidotti, "Limiting Occupational Medical Evaluations Under the Americans with Disabilities Act and the Genetic Information Nondiscrimination Act," *American Journal of Law and Medicine*, Vol. 41, No. 4, 2015, pp. 523–567.

Saks, Alan M., and Blake E. Ashforth, "Organizational Socialization: Making Sense of the Past and Present as a Prologue for the Future," *Journal of Vocational Behavior*, Vol. 51, No. 2, 1997, pp. 234–279.

Scherbaum, Charles A., Karen L. Scherbaum, and Paula Popovich, "Predicting Job-Related Expectancies and Affective Reactions to Employees with Disabilities from Previous Work Experience," *Journal of Applied Social Psychology*, Vol. 35, No. 5, 2005, pp. 889–904.

Seijts, Garard H., Daniel P. Skarlicki, and Stephen W. Gilliland, "Canadian and American Reactions to Drug and Alcohol Testing Programs in the Workplace," *Employee Responsibilities and Rights Journal*, Vol. 15, No. 4, 2003, pp. 191–208.

Serbu, Jared, "DoD Building Cyber Workforce of the Future," Federal News Radio, September 9, 2012.

Society for Industrial and Organizational Psychology, *Principles for the Validation and Use of Personnel Selection Procedures*, 4th ed., Bowling Green, Ohio, 2003.

Turner, Rhiannon N., Miles Hewstone, Alberto Voci, and Christiana Vonofakou, "A Test of the Extended Intergroup Contact Hypothesis: The Mediating Role of Intergroup Anxiety, Perceived Ingroup and Outgroup Norms, and Inclusion of the Outgroup in Self," *Journal of Personality and Social Psychology*, Vol. 95, No. 4, 2008, pp. 843–860.

United States Code, Title 10, Section 505, Regular Components: Qualifications, Term, Grade, last amended on October 14, 2008.

United States Code, Title 10, Section 532, Qualifications for Original Appointment as a Commissioned Officer, last amended on January 7, 2011.

U.S. Air Force, *USAF Medical Standards Directory (MSD)*, Washington, D.C., May 24, 2018.

U.S. Military Entrance Processing Command, "A Day at the MEPS," video transcript, 2017. As of September 19, 2018: http://www.mepcom.army.mil/Portals/112/Documents/DayattheMEPSVideoTranscript.pdf

Warner, John T., *Thinking about Military Requirement: An Analysis for the 10th QRMC,* Alexandria, Va.: CNA, 2008.

Wenger, Jennie W., Caolionn O'Connell, and Maria C. Lytell, *Retaining the Army's Cyber Expertise,* Santa Monica, Calif.: RAND Corporation, RR-1978-A, 2017. As of May 25, 2018:
https://www.rand.org/pubs/research_reports/RR1978.html

Wilkie, Robert L., "DoD Retention Policy for Non-Deployable Service Members," memorandum for Secretaries of the Military Departments, Chairman of the Joint Chiefs of Staff, Under Secretaries of Defense, Deputy Chief Management Officer, Chief, National Guard Bureau, and Director of Cost Assessment and Program Evaluation, Washington, D.C.: Office of the Under Secretary of Defense for Personnel and Readiness, February 14, 2018.

Yardley, Roland J., Peter Schirmer, Harry J. Thie, and Samantha J. Merck, *OPNAV N14 Quick Reference: Officer Manpower and Personnel Governance in the U.S. Navy—Law, Policy, Practice,* Santa Monica, Calif.: RAND Corporation, TR-264-NAVY, 2005. As of September 19, 2018:
https://www.rand.org/pubs/technical_reports/TR264.html